3000 800025 87415
St. Louis Community College

D1550705

APERTURE

NUMBER NINETY-ONE
SUMMER

2 **People and Ideas**
Good News: An Editorial
Pseudohistory/Pseudophotography: A Review of *Walker Evans at Work* and *Bearing Witness*, by Danny Lyon

4 **The Glamorous Art**
By Carter Ratcliff
What happened to Beauty? Art critic Carter Ratcliff finds it in the work of the seven photographers introduced in this issue.

8 **Nancy Hellebrand: More than a Face**
Moving in almost too close for comfort, Nancy Hellebrand makes portraits that reveal her subjects with startling intimacy.

14 **William Maguire: Night Light**
When the photographer steps out after dark, he sees a whole different world. William Maguire peers into the shadows of the night landscape.

24 **John Lueders-Booth: Inside Stories**
The persistence of self-identity is the underlying subject of John Lueders-Booth's portraits of women, taken in the Massachusetts Correctional Institution.

32 **Photography Comes of Age**
Frank Gohlke Interviews Ted Hartwell
Minneapolis photographer Frank Gohlke talks to Minneapolis Institute of Arts photography curator Ted Hartwell about the place of photography in public art collections.

40 **Stephen Scheer: America's Backyard**
Summer in small-town New England—Stephen Scheer captures the colors of Americans at leisure.

48 **Rhondal McKinney: Midwestern Moods**
Rhondal McKinney creates landscapes that are documents of the intense emotions aroused by certain combinations of light and terrain.

56 **Susan Barron: Beyond Collage**
Susan Barron photographs surreal assemblages put together from other pictures—one art transforms another.

62 **Michael Spano: City Rhythms**
Extending the camera's vision with multiple and wide-angle lenses, Michael Spano explores the effect of time in pictures of "cultural phenomena."

72 **Photography: Tradition and Decline**
By Carol Squiers
After reaching a height of popularity and prosperity in the 1970s, photography is in trouble. *Village Voice* writer Carol Squiers probes photography's history for the source of its present dilemma and a prescription for its future.

78 CONTRIBUTORS/CREDITS

Aperture (ISSN 0003-6420) is published quarterly, in February, May, August, and November, by Aperture, Inc., Elm Street, Millerton, New York 12546. A subscription for four issues is $32. Second Class Postage paid at Millerton, New York 12546. Postmaster: send address changes to Aperture, Elm Street, Millerton, New York 12546. A subscription for four issues outside the United States is $36. Because no publication of fine photography can be self-supporting in America, it is hoped that sponsors who wish to help maintain a vital force in photography will become Patrons ($1000), Donors ($500), Friends ($250), Sustaining Subscribers ($100), or Retaining Subscribers ($75). Names of Patrons, Donors, Friends, and Sustaining and Retaining Subscribers will appear in every issue for the duration of their sponsorship. Gifts (the donation less $32 for the subscription to *Aperture*) are tax deductible.
Single copies may be purchased for $12.50. ISBN 0-89381-127-0

People and Ideas

Good News: An Editorial

It is always good news when we can look to contemporary photography for pictures that enrich our experience. Too often we find ourselves drowning in what seems to be an endless stream of images—many of them stale repetitions of photographs we have already seen. While it is extremely difficult to make an original photograph, let alone a body of work that represents a consistent, exciting vision, it is easy to recognize a photograph that succeeds.

In the past decade we have probably all questioned whether anyone was making photographs that mattered. Many of us have left gallery exhibitions feeling let down. Some of us simply stopped going to exhibitions. Others waited patiently for the moment when the irrelevant would give way to the meaningful. The academic work that graced most museum and gallery walls in the past ten years probably signified a phase that photography had to get out of its system—the growing pains of a medium ideally suited for the contradictory demands of twentieth-century life: on the one hand, photography is the natural means of expression for our technological age; but, on the other hand, photography requires exceptionally talented individuals to employ its technology in the service of art.

Aperture has always opened its pages to new talent. In the early days the quarterly provided an outlet for the as yet unknown photographers Harry Callahan, Edward Weston, Frederick Sommer, Barbara Morgan, and Aaron Siskind, to name but a few. For this issue we asked curators, teachers, photographers, and our own contributing editors to recommend the best unknown, unpublished, or unexhibited photographers they knew, hoping to present our readers with a true discovery. Ultimately we reviewed over fifty portfolios to select the seven photographers—Susan Barron, Nancy Hellebrand, John Lueders-Booth, William Maguire, Rhondal McKinney, Stephen Scheer, and Michael Spano—whose work appears here. Each of them has produced a body of photographs that goes beyond the ordinary, reminding us of photography's potential for both insight and reflection.

THE EDITORS

Pseudohistory/Pseudophotography: A Review of *Walker Evans at Work* and *Bearing Witness*

When the poet Walt Whitman died in Camden, New Jersey, there were many close to him who took an intense interest in everything about him, for among the faithful he was an overwhelming figure. An autopsy was ordered and Whitman's brain was removed to be examined and preserved. But a laboratory technician dropped the brain of America's greatest poet on the floor. It broke into pieces and had to be discarded.

Walker Evans at Work is a book put together from Walker Evans's photographs and what one might call his "seconds" or "rejects." These are variations of his pictures that he chose not to publish but for which negatives were found in his files. Also reproduced are layouts he prepared while working at *Fortune* magazine and copies of layouts of his New York subway series. The text is made from notes, letters to and from him, unpublished writings, lists of equipment, copies of invoices, and excerpts from interviews—again much of it coming from Evans's own files. Although credit for the compilation and editing is not given on the title page, the effort seems to have been proposed by Frances Lindley, editor at Harper & Row, and endorsed by the Walker Evans estate. The rationalization for this colossal invasion of privacy is that since Evans dragged most of this stuff around with him his whole life, and did not destroy negatives, it can be assumed that he wanted his friends and executors to publish them. The mutilation of this country's finest photographer's work has been accomplished, according to the introduction by Jerry L. Thompson, "in the hope of showing something about how Walker Evans worked." But all the book does is to undermine the editing and privacy that Evans spent a lifetime establishing for his work and for himself. And it is done by and for the very people Walker Evans almost never photographed—people with an education.

Mr. Thompson's essay and the text present a man who could only have hated a book like this. When a student asked Walker Evans which camera he used to make a particular photograph, Evans answered that he resented the question, comparing it to asking a writer which typewriter he used. The student didn't get the answer, but we do. We are told that Mr. Evans had six SX-70s, that he in fact may not have known which camera he used to make the picture in question, and we are shown pictures made in the 1950s of him squatting and kneeling in front of a fire hydrant. Whoever is responsible for this might better have spent his or her time watching the presses run, because there was too much dirt on them and not enough ink.

A number of times Evans denounces the use of the word "documentary" to describe his work. In an 1971 interview he insists his is actually a "documentary style," "because documentary is police

Walker Evans, variant of *Phillipsburg, New Jersey*, 1936

Walker Evans, contact sequence of *Fulton Street, New York City*, 1929

photography of a scene of a murder" a style that Evans adopted. He is not making documents, he is using the style. Earlier, in a 1964 lecture, which for some reason is placed at the end of the book, Evans also denounces the word "documentary" and stresses the lyricism in his work. It is exactly that lyricism that this book so effectively undermines, and it does it in the guise of a documentary, but the only thing it actually documents is how a great photographer, and any photographer can be manipulated, undermined, and finally destroyed by the editing and presentation of "his work."

Visually, and that is a realm that Walker Evans occupied with undisputed honor, this book is a horror. Repeatedly pictures that have been known and loved for decades are reproduced beside variations of the same picture that Walker Evans made and rejected when he made them years ago. If Walker Evans wanted to change his mind and publish a different version, he had lots of time and plenty of opportunities to do it. But he didn't, and with good reason. Now that the question has been taken out of his hands, others have made the decision for him.

Photographs, no matter how great or how timeless, are made in a matter of moments. Both Evans and his friend James Agee have pointed out that the best photographs are sometimes made despite the intentions of the photographer. The rejects, and the errors, are made just as fast but, unlike other works of art, come forward not as sketches, plans, or drafts but as complete and finished works. They are, despite all the recent abuse, photographs. If a photographer as precise and determined as Walker Evans chose for decades to leave these things alone, what right does a Harper & Row editor have to unearth them now? This is not the same as showing us different versions of the Brooklyn Bridge, because no matter what the plans and sketches were, there is only one Brooklyn Bridge. That is almost never the case with a photograph.

The book in fact does not show "how Walker Evans worked." It only shows us how those responsible for this book work. Cicero is credited with having written Latin better than any other man, yet only one tenth of Cicero's works are thought to have survived and come down to us. What if, of all the fine books of Walker Evans' work, only this one were to survive? Would he still then have the stature he deserves? Perhaps posterity would think that Walker Evans was a company that employed and trained men, thirty or forty of which contributed to this book "in the documentary style." Even Cicero lost his head in the end. Walker Evans, the quintessential American, deserves a better fate.

In the book is a picture of the real Walker Evans at work made by his friend Paul Grotz in 1929. Looking at it I feel great affection for Walker Evans, who brought so much to our lives, and whose vision lives on, literally, in so many. He created America by seeing it the way he did. It was a great, powerful, proud, and democratic vision that he gave us. If they taught that at the universities, we'd all be a lot better off.

Michael Lesy's vision of America is

(continued on page 77)

The Glamorous Art

By Carter Ratcliff

Commenting on the Salon of 1859, Charles Baudelaire remarked, "Photography, like all other purely material developments of progress, [has] contributed much to the impoverishment of the French artistic genius." In Baudelaire's view, the fine arts of painting and poetry are synthetic. Photography's knack for "Truth" makes it analytic, and Truth, which we would call "objectivity," is repellent to "Beauty." As the photographic image promotes an "exclusive taste for the True," it "oppresses and stifles the taste of the Beautiful." Spared the knowledge of Louis Daguerre's and William Henry Fox Talbot's innovations, John Keats could ascend to the lyrical ecstasy of his "Ode on a Grecian Urn" of 1819, in which he writes that "Beauty is truth, truth beauty." Baudelaire, a later Romantic, felt that the camera's lens so grounded Truth in mundane fact that it had become the enemy of Beauty and our capacity to "create or feel wonder."

Some of Baudelaire's successors among Romantics and moderns tried to revive Keats's vision of truth's oneness with beauty, yet these efforts were increasingly desperate—which is to say ironic. Cubism's focus on the pictorial means by which painters since the Renaissance had devised their images of beauty represents the peak of that striving. In fact, the painter's devices are utterly conventional, unable to rise above their historical time and place to an unchanging realm of Truth with a capital *T*. Under pressure from Cubist analytics, beauty becomes exceedingly elusive. By 1920 T. S. Eliot could write of mundane fact accruing until it gains the weight of history, a labyrinth of the mind built of "cunning passages, contrived corridors/And issues," "a wilderness of mirrors" ("Gerontion"). Truth hides itself, and the search for beauty turns into an exercise in nostalgia.

Baudelaire's opposition of Truth to Beauty may seem glib, a too-easy consequence of his distaste for photographs, yet the 1859 Salon introduced an era when artists and writers found these ideals difficult to attain, impossible to unite. Edward Steichen's early, turn-of-the-century photographs, for example, sacrifice the objectivity of the medium to a brooding gauziness, a deliberate blurring borrowed from Symbolist painting's attempt to shield the memory of beauty from the glare of a mechanized age. Despite the hopes of Steichen and others, the serious photography of our century provides an immense dossier of evidence that Baudelaire was right: photographs cannot be works of art in the way that paintings (sometimes) are; the photograph militates against a traditional idea of beauty and hinders even our attempts to preserve that sense. A hostage of fact, photography can only mime a transcendent impulse.

Although Baudelaire cannot be applauded for excluding photography from the roster of art's important mediums, his claim that a painting is by its nature fundamentally different from a photographic print is a useful observation. Great ingenuity and a vast waste of talent have gone into the attempt to

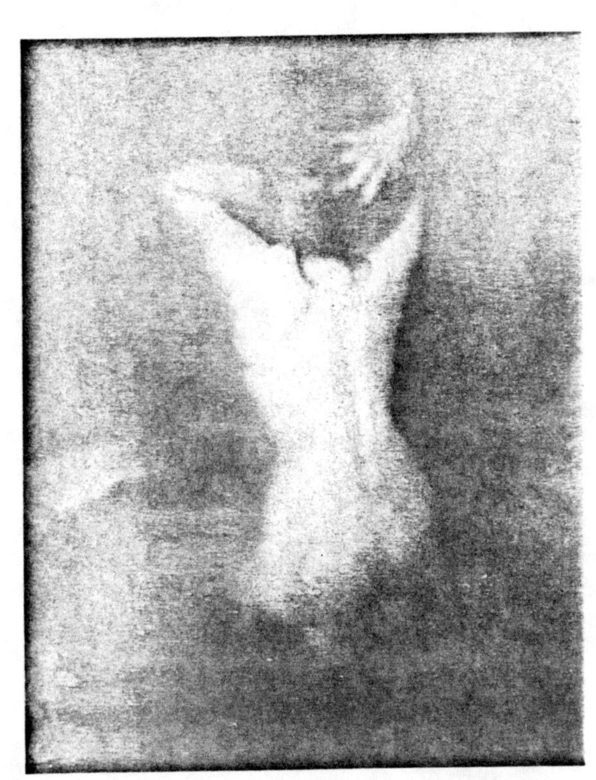

Edward Steichen, *Dolor*, April 1903. Photogravure

match photography with painting on the latter's own grounds. Steichen, László Moholy-Nagy, Ansel Adams, Man Ray, and a legion of others have entered this competition. Brilliant images appear, yet their brilliance is only rarely grasped, for photographers and their critics usually speak in terms more pertinent to paint on canvas. This obstinacy only dims our vision of the way photographs can be powerful. Composition, tonal nicety, color harmony—no matter how fully a photographer masters these formal attributes, they can never be as rich in his work as they are in a masterly painting; they are, at base, beside the photo-

graphic point. As for expressive force or psychological insight—a photograph offers these qualities in a manner exclusively its own. The coincidence that painting and photography are both visual mediums is irrelevant: painting resembles poetry more than it resembles photography, which is like theater.

Sometimes, when asked how long it took him to get an image, a photographer replies, "All my life." Obviously a lifetime of experience can go into a photograph. Just as obviously a photograph is the product of the instant during which an opened shutter transmits light through the lens to an emulsion. The eye perceives the photographic image in a reciprocal moment, all at once, in a flash of greater or lesser duration. Photographs very often reward extended contemplation, of course, but an image so contemplated never surrenders its air of instantaneity. A painting, as immediately striking as it may be, does not offer itself to the eye all at once and whole. Vision must ruminate over the painted surface before the viewer can fairly claim to have given it even a cursory look. (Admittedly, with practice, these ruminations can be swift.) Photorealist canvases may or may not provide exceptions here; the early Pop paintings of Andy Warhol and Roy Lichtenstein certainly do.

Warhol and Lichtenstein are masters of a variety of nonpainting: employing paint on canvas, they came up with images with the impact of photographs. In a way, they share a modernist goal with Edouard Manet, Paul Cézanne, and the Cubists, which is to unveil the premises of painting. Granted, the best Pop artists achieved a greater degree of radicalism; they undermined those premises completely, showing how an object that counts as painting could work like a photograph. Warhol and the rest were reviled, just as Baudelaire reviled the photographers of his day, for abandoning the eye to mundane reality, a dull Truth. They captured for painting a beauty alien to the medium, though long at home in photography despite photographers' yearnings for the beauties native to paint and canvas.

Warhol in particular found ways to make the painted image glamorous, and this was shocking. It still is. Glamour occurs when the mundane manages somehow to rise above itself, to take on an allure that everyday life denies it. Photography can achieve glamour by accident, as close perusal of almost any contact sheet reveals. Painting may capitalize on accidents, too, but its drawn-out processes insure that the medium's main thrust is deliberate and contemplative; hence our meditative approach to canvases. Jackson Pollock's supporters stress, quite rightly, the control he exerted over the paint he dripped and spattered and slung. Photographs of Pollock in the act of painting have glamour (and, in the case of Hans Namuth's prints, high aesthetic quality), whereas his paintings do not.

But are no paintings glamorous? Not when they are seen for what they are, although I agree that we often see them as something else—usually as icons of "serious" culture. One can recognize Rembrandt's *Aristotle Contemplating the Bust of Homer* out of the corner of one's eye, but in order to see what the artist intended the viewer must enter into the contemplation. Our first encounter with a painted image is soon forgotten, lost in the painstaking textures of the surface. Photographs permit no such forgetting. No matter how thoroughly Steichen's misty images of New York City entrance us, no matter how far or how long the eye is led into their depths, an atmosphere of immediacy, of the photographic instant, persists. Photographs show the ordinary drawn all of a sudden out of itself

Andy Warhol, *Close Cover Before Striking (Coca-Cola)*, 1962. Acrylic on canvas

and into the permanence of a perfect memory. This is indeed glamorous, and all the more powerful for that.

Those of us interested in the upper reaches of aesthetic possibility have a habit of dismissing glamour as trivial. Isn't it the domain of exploitative, throw-away imagery, the sort of stuff produced ad infinitum for the sake of entertainment, fashion, and the news? Yes, but no logic compels us to suppose that everything glamorous is suspect; and a body of photographic images, the product of nearly a century and a half of picture making, provides a great deal of evidence to the contrary. The glamour of which photography is capable presents us with something Baudelaire refused to see: a beauty specific to our technological age.

Glamour is spectacular. It offers the fiction that a theatrical climax can be sufficiently intense to detach itself from the flow of narrative, or simply from time, and exist forever in a state of visual immediacy. No painter's image has allure on the order of Lee Friedlander's *New York City*, 1964, his image of a man dozing at an office desk. The casual setting suggests Edward Hopper's paintings of the city, but Hopper pushed individuals toward archetype. Friedlander individualizes the typical, as do

even those photographers (Edward Weston, for instance) who try to find universal forms in the specific.

The thrust of modern painting—and of modern poetry, for that matter—comes from the failure of belief in universals. Faith fails, yet the desire to believe lingers on. Thus the painter's and the poet's ruminative, melancholy examination of premises and their ambiguities, the sifting through complexity that preoccupied the Cubists and T. S. Eliot. In our time, painting and poetry have been radical insofar as they looked backward, with regret, at what art has lost to a technological age. In this nostalgic posture, these mediums have stood apart from ordinary life, offering refuge. Photography and its theatrical offspring, film, do the opposite.

Constitutionally unfit for the propagation of universals, photography and film immerse themselves in the contingencies, the chaos, of the modern world. Despite the ostensible high-mindedness of Edward Weston's motives, for example, his images of bell peppers are valuable precisely to the extent that they do not

Edward Weston, *Cabbage Leaf*, 1931

attain the status of Platonic archetypes. Unbeknown to himself, Weston was as interested in the contingent as, say, Robert Frank. Photography must begin with what is, not with what might be or what, in the hidden light of a poetic sensibility, ought to be. It is a medium predicated on acceptance. Thus photography and the movies are our hopeful mediums, especially when they show a positive side to those qualities so often scorned—theatricality and glamour.

Glamour flashes, but its surface brilliance does not preclude complexity—far from it. Photography is a sudden embrace impelled by passions, and the forms it produces can be intricate indeed. To reverse Baudelaire's judgment, photographs are syntheses. They bring artist, subject, and viewer together in a focused burst of light. Painting and poetry have turned out to be our analytic mediums, disassembling form and meaning until they risk getting lost in Eliot's "wilderness of mirrors." Photography's synthesizing impulses can be observed in examples from any of the last ten or twelve decades, but they have never been more apparent than in the work of photographers today, including those whose work is reproduced here.

William Maguire approaches his subjects with theatrical instincts (pages 14–23). His photographs of small Florida towns at night read like stage sets. Clear form joins even clearer perspectives; in other words, these very ordinary buildings, angular shapes of clapboard and stucco, line up dramatically along streets set at striking angles to the plane of the image. Lighting appears to have been carefully arranged to catch textures that in turn catch the eye. But, of course, this is not the case. Maguire records actualities, not a set designer's effects. There is much social, even sociological, commentary in his work. Such content could be conveyed in a variety of mediums, however, from academic prose to realist painting. The specifically photographic meanings come from the images' deep grounding in fact. Maguire shows us the mundane asserting itself against its own negligibility, and glamour is the result—not a trivial celebration of local color but a somber acceptance of places and, by implication, ways of life all too easy to dismiss. As he says, "It is not the photographer's problem to interpret or to arrange artfully." In these photographs, banal and dilapidated buildings serve as emblems of a daily round whose dignity is so secret and dubious that it can only flash forth at night.

Maguire's effects require the stage to be cleared. Stephen Scheer treats his locales as backdrops for people (pages 40–47). He seems to have felt at home in The Maples, a Connecticut town along the Housatonic River, though he wisely leaves it unclear just how much an outsider he remained. People often look at him and his camera, but never as if they were turning to a member of the family. Scheer's intention was documentary, he says, and he shares with us our inevitable distance from his subject. Men, women, and children present themselves to the lens, sometimes with a carefully calculated degree of indifference. The artist uses his camera to alert the residents of The Maples to themselves—to their singularity, on the one hand, and on the other to their places in a network of social usage and ceremony. One feels dailiness becoming conscious of itself in a series of privileged moments—not that routine is broken, but that its purpose, the point of these ordinary lives, manages to rise a bit closer to the surface than usual.

The world of John Lueders-Booth's photographs is a prison, a place where routine is imposed (pages 24–31). An individual can hardly accept this imposition, only attempt to survive in the face of it. The women in the Framingham prison suffer a contradiction. Their lives are relentlessly boring and yet their very selves are always at stake. These prisoners came to trust Lueders-Booth; nonetheless, taking up a pose even for him is an act rigid with tension. His camera presents a challenge, an instant of confrontation. Some of the Framingham women enter

this drama equipped with conventional emblems of glamour—signs that their sexiness, their personal authority, their resemblance to people on the outside cannot be killed off. But the power of these photographs doesn't depend on the vexed allure of their subjects. It is the result of Lueders-Booth's ability to

Robert Frank, *Man Reading Newspaper in Window*, c. 1960

precipitate the moment when self-image begins to reveal self, and the posture a prisoner assumes in order to do her time turns into an image of a life history.

Michael Spano's Graph-Check sequence camera brings the flow of cinematic time to still photography. With his Widelux camera, Spano compresses time into an instant of expansiveness (pages 62–71). People loom up to and away from the camera. Form blurs. Space sometimes seems to be molded by the gravity and the gestures of those who occupy it. Spano's is an art of currents and countercurrents, not of resolutions. He talks of "rhythm," not of the conclusions to which rhythms lead, and he immerses us in time rather than takes us out of it. Nonetheless, for all their shifts in scale and their extreme spatial tensions, these photographs are whole. They are like the afterimages of a spectacle so fast-moving and intimate the eye could hardly see it when first unrolled. Spano's camera shows us instants in the life of a subject normally unseeable, which goes by the name of atmosphere or ambiance.

In search of textures specific to her art, Nancy Hellebrand moves in very close to faces (pages 8–13). These pores and wrinkles are, of course, immediately decipherable. We know how faces look. With astonishing thoroughness, Hellebrand has translated that knowledge into a photographic mode. Details so familiar one hardly sees them in ordinary life take on the immediacy of the just discovered. Hellebrand alienates us from the well-known in order to return us to it. Her most important resource is a limitation of her 8 x 10 camera—its shallow field of focus. This restriction of the camera's eye isolates clarity between regions of blurring. Framed by the edges of the prints, the softened contours of a face frame selected views of high, sharp focus. Hellebrand translates each subject's presence into terms that are exclusively visual. Texture is less tactile than retinal here: she doesn't deny other terms—those of touch, of the psyche, and so on; she absorbs them all in the instant of seeing. In Hellebrand's images, the grain of skin blends with the silver-nitrate grain of the print—the photograph's own skin.

Much the same happens in Rhondal McKinney's midwestern landscapes (pages 48–55). The textures of his world are those of plowed earth, drifted snow, bare and distant trees against milky skies. Print quality evokes the quality of long-distance seeing, for McKinney joins the random photochemical processes of the medium to the sweeping, always deliberate impulses of his eye. What is accidental, a matter of substances interacting with light, becomes impossible to distinguish from the intentional. This union occurs whenever photography achieves the fullness of art, and we note it in an instant—that moment in which the eye reenacts the synthesizing gesture of the camera. The result is a burst of theater that transcends the theatrical, that stands outside the pressures of time and day-today narrative to epitomize some aspect of the here and now. This is the source of glamour in the best, most challenging sense of the word, one that can apply to the photocollages of Susan Barron (pages 56–61).

Collage developed out of the analytic pressures painting exerted on itself in the early decades of this century. It mocks the modernist painter by suggesting that only fragmentation is possible—why not just assemble scraps of ready-made imagery? Collage is an elegiac medium, born out of the ruins of the hope that painting could, in the twentieth century, recover its premodern unity. Barron changes this mood abruptly. She assembles her works from image fragments. They are filled with the contradictions, the ambiguities, the "cunning passages" we expect from collage. Yet these are not collages. They are photographs. Their surfaces are smooth and whole. They offer us not disintegration to be contemplated but totalities to be grasped all at once.

In the face of modernist irony and its difficulties, Barron has created images of the ironic. Irony presents itself here as an option, not a psychic or historical necessity. The sheer assertiveness of the photographic image seems to present a way out of modernism's inward-turning labyrinth, its reflexiveness. Hence the medium's optimism, which underlies even the most horrific picture. Photography confronts the world directly (once Barron shoots her collages, even these very private works take on a thoroughly public presence), and out of that directness come a truth and beauty peculiar to our times.

Nancy Hellebrand: More than a Face

I have been photographing people for twenty years. At times the pictures were portraits, at times street pictures. Always I took many pictures of someone, but would show only one because I "knew" I could take only a single definitive photograph of a person. Now, working with portraits again, I "know" that each situation or moment in a life has many aspects and that many things are true at the same time.

I use an 8 x 10-inch camera to get large pictures without the graininess of an enlargement. I want to look very closely at someone's face and I want to see skin, not dots. Placing the camera very close to the subject magnifies the face. Subtle and unexpected areas become prominent. New priorities are established. Watching the features on the ground glass becomes a process of recognition—the person is revealed—the face becomes a picture.

Joy, 1982

Carlos, 1982

onnie, 1982

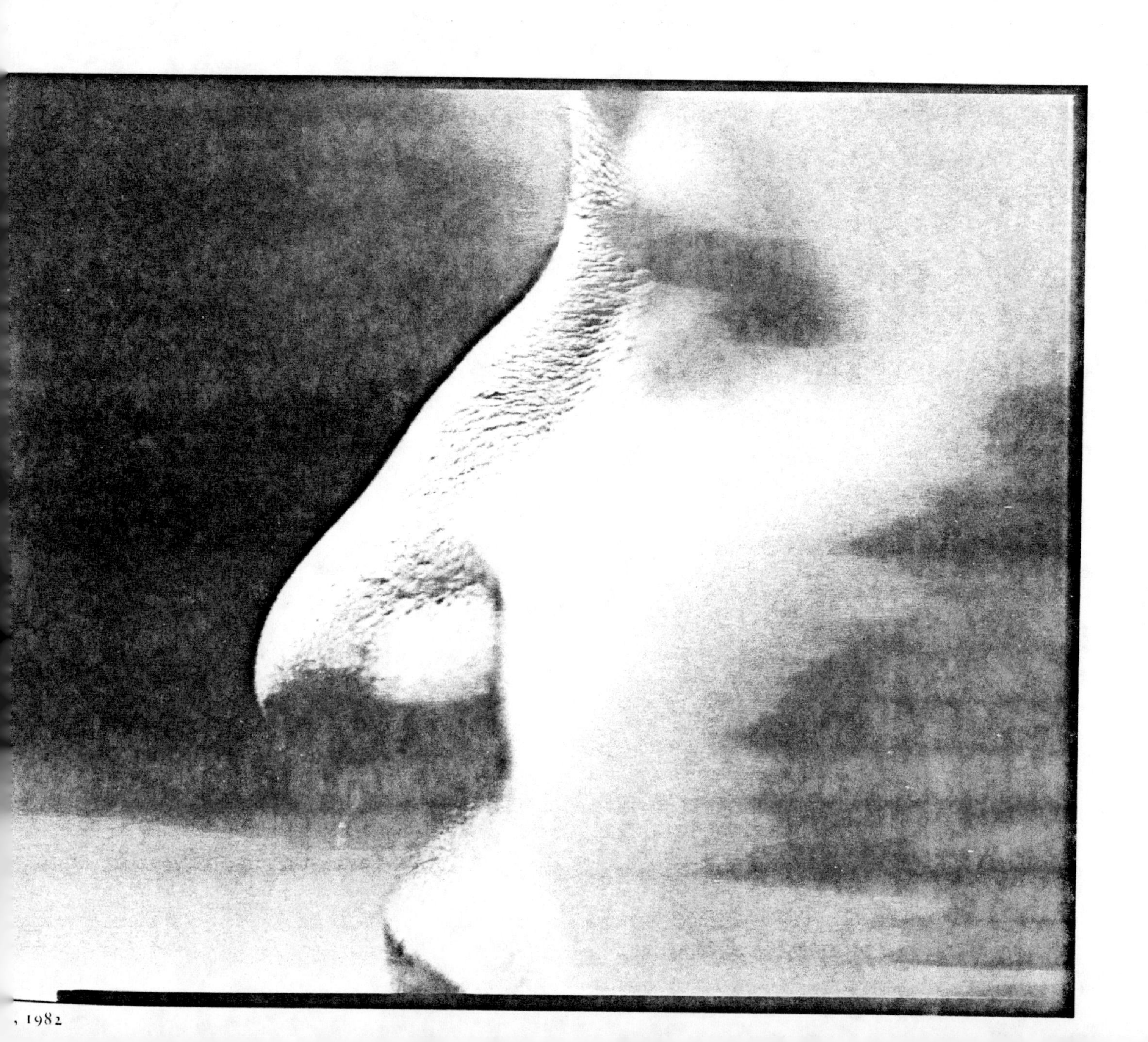

, 1982

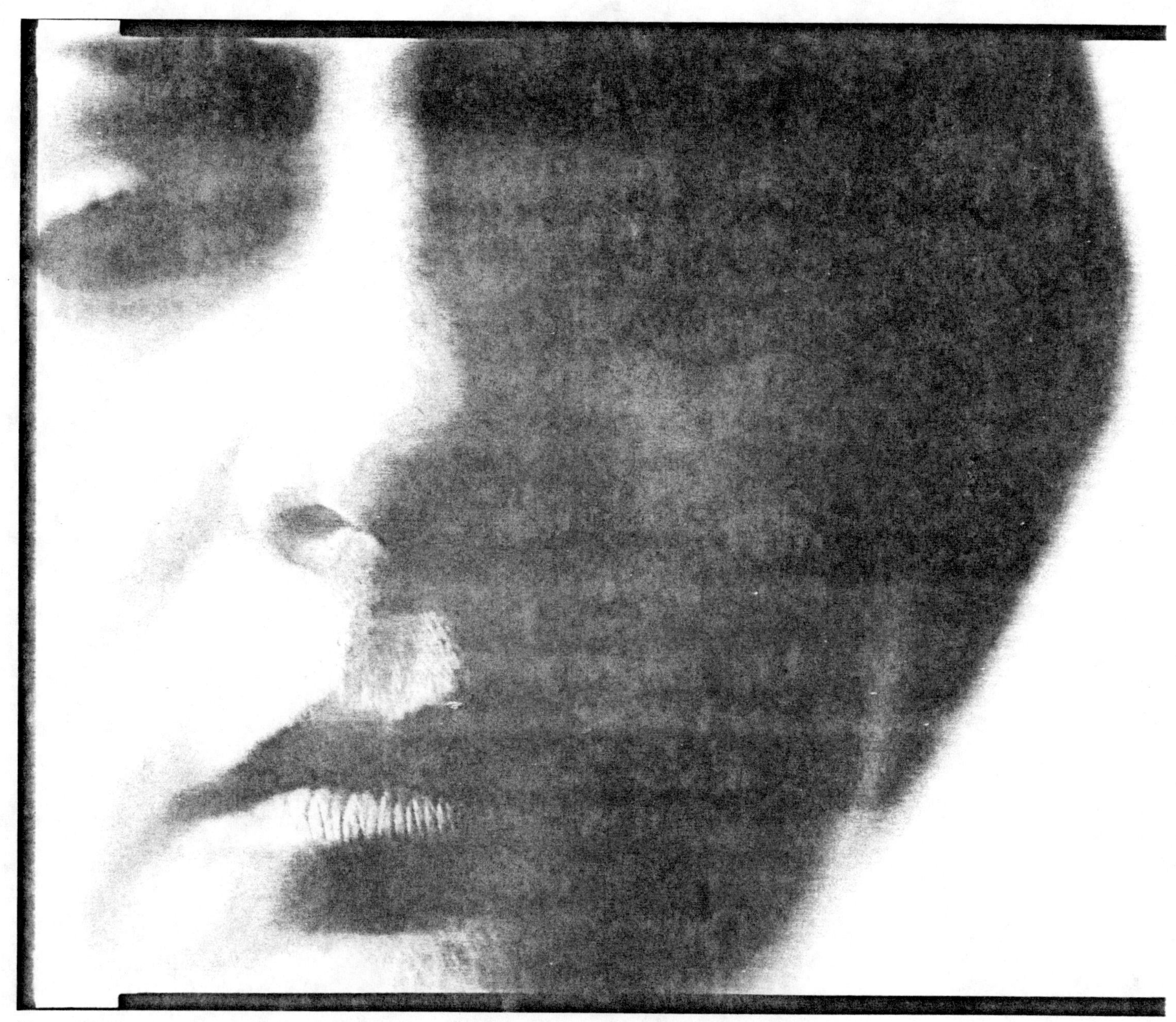

Margo, 1982

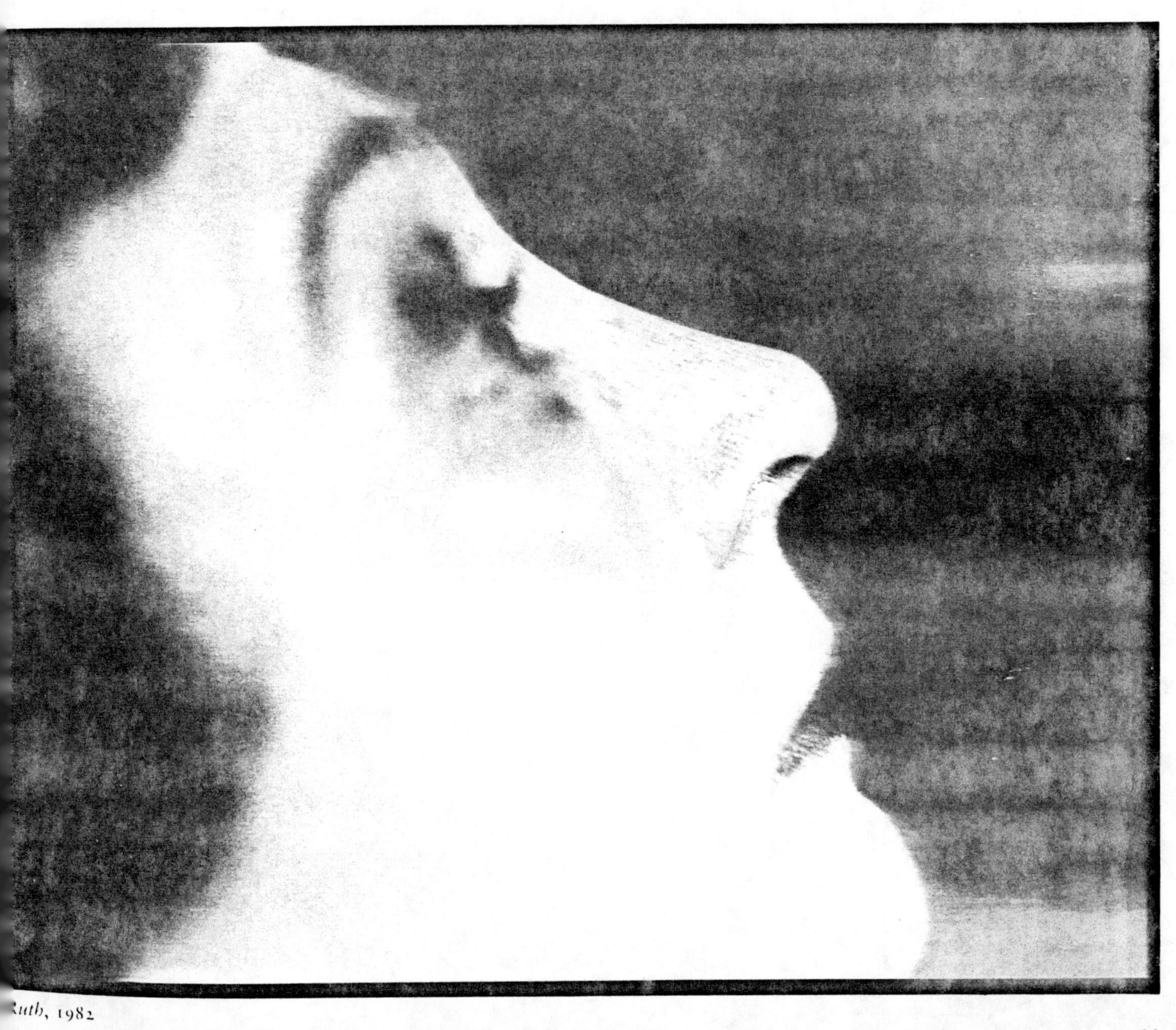

Ruth, 1982

William Maguire: Night Light

Anyone who is interested in how things look notices how something ordinary is beautifully transformed by light. Light draws attention to what it describes.

I am interested in how a beautiful photograph defies interpretation: how it may be ripe in implication and surface, yet free of conventional meaning. It is not the photographer's problem to interpret or to arrange artfully. Any impulse to fool arbitrarily with the form means the work is no longer contending with the act of seeing. The form has to be intensely beautiful without in the least drawing attention to itself.

A photographer who understands the illusionistic nature of the medium knows that you have to describe the subject even more richly than the eye can see, yet remain faithful to the eye's way of seeing. If I look at a building at night, I can see into all of its shadows and brightly lit areas. If the place is beautiful in dramatic light, then the full, rich range of detail is part of why it is interesting to see.

Photography is constricted by its essential descriptive nature. There is little room for innovation or experimentation. Paradoxically, the most radical activity is clothed in acceptance of a convention and a tradition.

These night photographs are not the product of any idea but of taking a kind of chance. Almost always, I did not realize what was there. The reward can far exceed the risk.

Joe's, New Orleans, 1975

JOE'S
GROCERY & SWEET
SHOP
Coca-Cola
SIGN OF GOOD TASTE

Facade, New Orleans, 1976

NO PARKING

Church near Masonic Hall, Princeton, Florida, 1974

J.A. Kelley, Georgia, 1978

J.A.KELLEY AND CO.

Overhang, New Orleans, 1977

Girod

John Lueders-Booth: Inside Stories

The Massachusetts Correctional Institution at Framingham is a special prison. It is a women's prison, the first in the country. Founded in 1879, it served to incarcerate unmarried women for "begetting" (Hester Prynne's crime in *The Scarlet Letter*). Now it imprisons them for, among other things, shoplifting, organized prostitution, using and trafficking in heroin and other drugs, armed robbery, and murder. Many women at Framingham were convicted for helping their husbands or boyfriends commit crimes. Many of them have done time before, and many have dependent children who are in the care of relatives or court-appointed foster parents.

In the fall of 1977 I went to the Framingham prison to set up and teach a photography class. In the course of this work I began photographing the inmates. For the next four years I continued to go to Framingham three or four days a month to make photographs and to teach.

JEAN

Photography Comes of Age

Frank Gohlke Interviews Ted Hartwell

Ted Hartwell is curator of photography at The Minneapolis Institute of Arts. Frank Gohlke is a photographer who lives in Minneapolis.

FG *As the director of a very important photography collection—the person who takes care of it, adds to it, the person who really created it—how do you see your responsibilities? What kind of decisions do you have to make in running the day-to-day operations of the collection and its more ephemeral counterpart, the exhibition program?*
TH I've always seen the exhibition program and the selection and ultimate purchase of photographs for the collection as complementary activities. In principle, I believe that anything I put on the wall for an exhibition I could also be proud to add to the collection. Each exhibition year I try to intersperse historical with contemporary material—the relatively unknown and altogether unknown photographer, both contemporary and historical, with the well-known figures, Edward Weston, Ansel Adams, and Eugène Atget, for example. This makes it possible to draw connections between contemporary and earlier work.
FG *Why is that important, do you think?*
TH I think that's the way we understand art. That's the way we understand anything we do, as human beings, by connecting and relating, by making cross-references. But that process presumes first of all that there is an audience out there who will be interested in those connections.
FG *Who do you think that audience is?*
TH Ideally, the audience I have in mind knows every bit as much about photography as I do—in many cases, maybe more than I do. Therefore, I am challenged to do the very best in making an intelligent selection, thinking carefully about the presentation. Traditionally, that ideal audience has been made up of photographers, but I also have to consider the museum professionals. My museum colleagues have, with good cause, many serious and carefully considered reservations about whether photography belongs in a museum. I feel I must demonstrate that photographs are worthy of being on museum walls.
FG *Do you really think they have good cause?*
TH Well, in the absence of a long and considered history of the medium of photography, there are many issues that haven't been as fully explored as, say, in Italian painting of the eighteenth century. It is interesting that a curator at a major museum, which has a major photography collection, still in some way feels he has to argue for, or keep up a constant lobbying for, the legitimacy of his medium, even though it commands a substantial part of the museum's exhibition space. I'm sure that my gnawing sense of inadequacy comes from feeling that I don't know as much as I want to know. I would love to have at my disposal all the artillery of the classically trained art historian in the service of defending, if that's the proper term, my medium of choice. I stand in awe of the art historians I've grown up with in the museum business. I have enormous regard for their scholarship.

I'm not saying that I have to defend any purchase or any photograph, but too often, I think, photography has been discussed in terms that don't have the force and eloquence of considered knowledge.
FG *That is a complaint that has been voiced for a long time, but only in the last five or ten years has the lack of a body of substantial critical thought come to be seen as so glaring, so important. It's not a question of quality; it's a question of depth. Rank upon serried rank of diligent to indolent scholars are all plugging away at the history of painting. There is something almost horrifying about it. At the same time, an army like that is something to be reckoned with, even if most of what they produce is drivel.*
TH It's a great challenge, not to say that it's a burden, to sponsor candidates for inclusion in the history of photography. When I sit on committees with the rest of the staff, I don't think that there is any doubt in the minds of any of my colleagues that the work I acquire is substantial and does indeed have the weight and authority that I claim it has. I don't think it's a case of the Emperor's New Clothes. The work I present I defend convincingly, and the evidence is indeed the work.
FG *Apart from weight and substance, can you articulate the principles or criteria that guide your selection of the photographs you put before your committee and before the public? Do you have a theory of the medium that guides you, or is it more of an intuitive process?*
TH It's largely intuitive, but the intuitive response is formed by immersion in the images and literature of our field—primarily images. I can fit any given image into a relationship with other images that I hold in the back of my mind. I also look for

indicators that show that the photographer has considered the meanings that reside or are available in the subject, and has responded to them with economy, intelligence, compassion, and sensitivity; that the dialogue between photographer and subject adds to what we already know about the medium, rather than mirrors what we've already seen. I have no scale, no absolute yardstick. One can fall back on all sorts of catchwords—balance, harmony, rhythm, structure—but my evaluation of a photograph primarily has to do with its relationship to the work that by consensus we admire.

FG *But that sounds so self-contained, self-enclosed. Do you ever encounter work by photographers who are in some way really outside* the *field—but whom you somehow can't ignore?*

TH Yes, I guess I consciously look for work that goes against the grain, that doesn't have a predetermined place within the set of assumptions we call the history or aesthetics of photography. I am really drawn to publications like *Interview* magazine, and some of the rock-and-roll magazines that are full of a crazy energy that doesn't come from a conscious understanding of, say, Edward Weston or André Kertész.

FG *Do you ever solicit work from people whose work you see in magazines like that?*

TH A lot of it comes in when people call and ask to bring in portfolios.

FG *Do you also go out and look at things?*

TH It's a combination. One of the big questions is whether looking at work is the best use of my time. Is that what a curator is supposed to do? I might be able to say yes. It may have been Walter Hopps, director of the Menil Collection in Houston, who said that if a curator is in his office, he's not doing his job. I should be out in people's studios. I should be going through picture files. Henry Geldzahler had a wonderful thing to say in a recent issue of *Interview* about why he left The Metropolitan Museum of Art. He said he became disconnected from what he thought was most vital in contemporary art. I think that's a bit dramatic. The way I handle it is that when someone calls and says, "How do you do this? Can I bring work and show it to you?"—I say, "Because of the demands on my time, I'd like to ask you to bring your work, leave it with me, and I'll call you after I've had a chance to look at it. I won't promise that I can talk with you about it, unless it's appropriate. But I will look at it. I can promise you that. Please don't get your heart set on a result from this—either exhibition or purchase—because that may or may not happen." I've had to draw the line at student work, though. I've always felt that my colleagues in the teaching community were providing that instruction. But, with the exception of students, I look at everybody's work.

I'm leery about publicizing my availability, because I'm just one person. And I am also trying to raise money and put together a catalogue of the collection, and it is a simple matter of how best to use my time. Of course, often the most effective use of my time *is* sitting down and helping a photographer come to terms with his or her work, clarifying things. It is important for me to articulate what I see so that it makes sense to the picture maker.

When I went to New York and worked with Eve Sonneman, she had ten years of photographs to sort through for her Minneapolis exhibition. It took a couple of days just to go through it all, and she stood silently. She didn't involve herself, except to bring more work to me. There I was just plowing through her photographs and setting things aside. What was particularly gratifying, and most valuable from her point of view, was that I was making choices that coincided with the way she saw her work. The process of selecting provided fresh insights for her. Because she had respect for what I was doing and watched carefully, my combinations, selections, or rejections of pictures were meaningful. She was then able to decide which work she had hesitations about and which she was really committed to. In this new combination, she suddenly discovered something that she had never thought about in her work. And I discovered things, too.

FG *You let your hand do it, and then your mind realized what your hand had done?*

TH Yes, in putting together an exhibition I want to suspend preconceptions that might unfairly condition the selective process. In a way it's selfish, because my primary motivation is to know the work, and to test myself. I remember when I was a photography student how badly I wanted to see original prints. In the ten years that I've been heading this collection I have been able to get those pictures, touch them, preserve them, and share them with a community that appreciates them. I can't tell you how exciting that is.

FG *You work in an art museum, and everything that appears in the museum is presumed to be art. Obviously, most of the billions of photographs made every year don't fit your definition of art—at least the institution's definition of art. And yet some images not intended as art end up on museum walls. The implication is that because they are now on the museum walls they are now art. Exhibiting them changes their status. Do you ever feel you've put on the walls of your museum images that really might appropriately be better seen somewhere else? Or images that are somehow seriously distorted by that context?*

TH Yes, sometimes the context of an exhibition can lead you to conclude that an image that is not art is every bit as good as anything else on the museum walls. And that's dangerous. But I don't think anybody is going to be forever damaged or corrupted by an exhibition, and I think there are ways of qualifying what you show, with explanatory wall labels, for example.

FG *In the current exhibition of photography at The Minneapolis Institute of Arts,* Pictorialism in America: The Minneapolis Salon Photographers, 1932–1946, *an exhibition of amateur photography in Minneapolis during the 1930s and 1940s, there are many pictures that do not conform to current standards of what is artistically significant in form or content. Your wall space is limited; your calendar is very limited. Hundreds of young photographers see those walls as a kind of Promised Land to which they hope to be admitted, and many fine photographers in this area deserve to be shown. What do you see as the justification of putting up a show like this?*

TH Well, in the first place, as much as I'm devoted to looking at new work and trying my best to find it, nourish it, encourage it, and ultimately display and buy it, I believe I have a responsibility to the history of the medium, and I think an exhibition like this one, although I didn't create it—Christian Peterson is the curator—is a very worthy one. It's a chronicle of an era, the taste of a period. It represents in compressed and heavily edited form an attitude about photography that has enjoyed great currency in this country.

FG *So it's really about the history of taste?*

TH Yes, it is a way of looking carefully at a particular period. The Minneapolis Camera Club was very active, but like most camera clubs it was at variance with certain ideas and attitudes

Paul L. Anderson, *Vine in Sunlight*, 1944, from *Pictorialism in America*

that have enjoyed the sanction of arts organizations, art critics, and art historians. If younger photographers see this exhibition today and say, "What? How dare you put that crap up on the walls?," I think that's wonderful. I think that's something to learn from, too. Further, I want to appeal to the photographers and the families who lent pictures to donate their work to the museum as the Minneapolis Camera Club Collection.

FG *That raises a lot of interesting issues. What does it say, for example, about the nature of photography as a cultural phenomenon that an exhibition of such photography can be justified, while the idea of having a comparable show of Sunday painters is inconceivable? What is the difference?*

Adolf Fassbender, *City, Thy Name Be Blessed*, 1937, from *Pictorialism in America*

TH The difference is in the ways painting and photography deal with images. With photography, you know the case is not closed. The history is still being written, and many photographs and photographers deserve to be reconsidered.

FG *Let me ask you a couple of impertinent questions. Number one, at any time was there any problem getting approval for this exhibition?*

TH No.

FG *Do you ever have to clear your exhibitions?*

TH Oh yes, always. I have to present a proposal to a committee of curators, including the director and the chief curator.

FG *Do you think that the approval of this show had anything to do with trustees having been Camera Club members or with the fact that the exhibition may be a popular success and bring a good many people into the museum who might not otherwise come to it?*

TH Such considerations absolutely had a bearing on our decision to do the show. In this case, the main concern was not to make a particular point about the aesthetic validity or merit of the show or of the individual pictures. The Centennial of the Society of Fine Arts was in 1982, and the exhibition can be seen as part of the history of the museum.

FG *Because the Camera Club held a salon every year?*

TH Exactly. For years there was an annual exhibition of this very nature at the museum. It was hard-core amateur photography of its time, part of a tradition. So, in looking at ourselves on the occasion of the Centennial, we revived the format, in some cases hanging the very pictures that were on the walls in 1939. It may be a bit nostalgic, a little self-indulgent, and, not to put too fine a point on it, the exhibition flatters some of the people who were involved seriously and emotionally with the camera clubs in those days. Some of those people are our trustees, and it will please them. I don't think that's a bad thing. In many cases these people hadn't thought about those pictures for forty years, and it pleases me to be able to remind them of their former interest, and to remind them that times have changed. Today photographs are looked at and evaluated and collected according to different criteria.

The response to this show will be from an audience that has, for the most part, silently disapproved of some of the exhibitions that I've had. Now they are pleased that their kind of photography is being shown again—the kind of photography that we associate with the gravure section of the Sunday newspaper of the 1940s and 1950s, or landscapes like the view across Lake Harriet at sunset. It puts things in perspective. But that may not be a good enough reason to use that wall space for pictures that really can't be justified according to our present standards.

FG *Do you feel you are being used to mollify a certain section of the public?*

TH I'm not sure much harm is done. I don't think we're lowering our high standards by doing an exhibition that in some ways is a rather flagrant denial or contradiction of our present criteria. I think maybe it's so flagrant that it's evident what's going on, and that's okay.

FG *For some people it will be, and for some it won't.*

TH Well, what I would hope is that the people who really want to challenge the exhibition will speak out and make their views known. I'd like to see some clearly stated letters, both pro and con. I'm not at all opposed to mounting exhibitions that will throw the audience a curve. Frankly, I expected hostile reactions to the Paul Outerbridge exhibition. Some of his pictures—for example, the guy at the coffee machine with the housewives around it—are just the dumbest kind of advertising illustration, and there is hardly any excuse for putting that kind of picture on the walls. I remember when our chief curator walked through this show with me, he stopped by the coffee-machine picture and said, "We can't show this. It's terrible. It's just trivial. Look at that. The color is wrong. It's dumb. It's just a hopeless picture." And I said, "But, within the context of the exhibition, it tells us a lot about the taste of the period, the diversity of this man's activity. We can come to all sorts of conclusions about the cultural context of these images." It's very different from putting up some extraordinary spare and austere Harry Callahan prints, but I can't condemn the Outerbridge or Pictorial photographers shows. They have a certain naïveté, a certain innocence, but I guess temperamentally I'm given to a certain tolerance for things like that.

FG *I think we are really caught between conflicting definitions of what a museum is. Museums are really quite recent, but we tend to behave as though they have always existed and people have always used them in the same way as they use them now. I think that the confusion about the function of museums is particularly acute in the case of photography, which we're still in the process of trying to figure out. What is this tool we have? Is it in fact our tool anymore? Are we its creature to a greater degree than it is ours? Are you, as a museum curator, necessarily an educator? Is it your function to attract and educate and woo a larger audience for photography as a fine art, as if that were somehow what photography had always aspired to? Or are you merely a kind of index or reporter to a select community interested in photography as it is used by people who think of themselves as artists? Is your primary responsibility to define an art historical tradition of the medium or to break that tradition open at every opportunity you can? It seems to me that a lot of the conundrums that one confronts as a curator of photography in a major museum are really indicative of photography's unsettled position in the culture at large, and its uneasy and uncomfortable adaptation to a context formed according to art historical principles that were only invented a hundred or a hundred twenty-five years ago. In some ways art history is even younger than photography, and yet we speak of painting as having a "great tradition," as if the tradition were synonymous with art history's version of it. Certainly painting has always had a tradition. Painters have known it. Painters have* lived *it. But the idea of people other than painters specializing in the study of art history, that's relatively new.*

TH All the aspects you've mentioned about functioning within a museum are very real. It is a balancing act. You vacillate between creating exhibitions that please a wide public and those that deal with concerns specific to the picture maker. I identify closely with the picture maker, because I came to the field as a photographer. I still play with a Polaroid SX-70 and fancy that I'm forming a personal vision, which I hope doesn't obscure or obstruct the way I respond to other people's work. But it's another matter to present exhibitions that are not only well received by an informed audience but are also popular and help raise the head count. In all fairness, a museum has to justify its existence to the individuals, agencies, and corporations that support it. That's not to say that the high artistic and scholarly purposes served by first-rate exhibitions, regardless of how many people see them, are not important. Museum administrators respect the finer, subtler, more elusive, and less quantifiable aspects of the museum—the high purposes—but they know at the same time that it's virtually impossible to go to the Minnesota state legislature with the request for the annual subsidy unless you can prove that you are serving the public. And you measure the public by the number of people you have coming through the museum.

Actually, serving the larger audience has also always been an exciting thing for me. The most uninformed of gallery visitors can look at an exhibition, and if I've done my job in structuring and pacing it, and making it a pleasant thing to look at, then they'll go away feeling that they know more or have a better sense of what photography is than when they entered.

FG *Do you think they know more about the particular work itself?*

TH That's a little more than I can do, but I'd like to believe that they know more about themselves. To put those things up there is to aspire to make the viewers better people. I know all sorts of terrible things have been foisted upon the public in the name of personal improvement—it's a dangerous thing even to touch on—but it is still one of the things I think about when I am putting up a show.

FG *Well, who knows what makes people better? What we might be able to hope for is that people leave an exhibition having discovered that there is a source of experience available to them that they didn't realize was there before—a whole class of objects in the world capable of yielding a great deal more than they had ever given them credit for.*

But let's get back to the question of judgment and taste. You have said that Lee Friedlander, Walker Evans, and Eugène Atget are really at the center of your own personal conception of photography.

TH They ring truest for me. The forms that their pictures take seem to be the most economical, to provide the most lucid kind of visual exposition; they're models for that. But I can't use that as the archetype for assessing work of a different nature. For example, the Edward Steichen gravures in *Camera Work* are so strongly Victorian, it doesn't make any sense to expect them to conform to a more austere aesthetic.

FG *Can you put aside what really moves you and touches you in the most profound way in order to try to understand something that works on different principles?*

TH I guess I try to meet a photograph on its own terms. I assume that if something is offered as a serious artistic statement, it is seriously intended.

FG *You mentioned your experience working with Eve Sonneman. Do you generally find that the presence of the artist is helpful in understanding his or her work?*

TH It can cloud the issue. When I have the photographer standing right there as I look at the work, I'm always inclined to find something positive to say.

FG *All right. Let's say you get a batch of things in front of you that you've never seen before. What do you look for?*

TH I guess I always look for a way into the material, to see what it is, not to go to it with a lot of expectations. I certainly expect to find *something,* and I hope to find something of substance. But I try to meet it on its own terms and mentally check off points at which it fails or succeeds. Is it well executed? That's an easy one. You can say, "This looks like a student print" or "This is not very well handled"—the photographer's experience with the materials, whatever they are. Then, how well does that image convey its intention? If it's a photograph of a building or a person, how well situated was the camera in relation to the subject? What is the photographer's personal relationship to that thing or that place out there? Is it well considered? Is it carefully seen?

FG *What if the work has nothing to do with being careful?*

TH If it's loose and gestural and haphazard, then I ask myself if, in its denial or disregard of those virtues or those other qualities, it is a convincing or an authentic expression. Does it ring true? Does it affect me? Is it similar to something else I have seen? I rifle instantly through the catalogue of images in the back of my head to see if it fits anywhere.

FG *What if it doesn't?*

TH If it doesn't, then I look a second time. I say to myself, this is a new creature. What is it? What are its elements? Do those elements convey a new observation? Is there something fresh going on here? Or is it just a glib exercise? Does it seem sincere as an expression of a sentiment or energy? Or is it facile? If it's something that really eludes any attempt to place or connect it, I go through the exercise of creating a kind of mini-exhibition. In my office, pictures and frames are stacked everywhere. If I see something that really throws me a curve, I like to reach down for a Manuel Alvarez Bravo or an August Sander or a Lee Friedlander and put it next to the new image as a sort of spur-of-the-moment contest. It helps me think.

Usually, when I'm looking at some photographer's work in his or her presence, I'll find myself doing a lot of that sort of juxtaposition. I don't mean such comparisons to be put-downs, but I think photographers should know the other pictures that look like theirs, not to avoid being accused of simple recapitulation or thoughtless emulation but in order to be able to use what the other work has to offer. So the collection as a didactic tool is terrifically important to the way I function, the way I think. It's almost impossible for me to talk to young photographers about their work unless they have some grounding in the contemporary history of photography.

FG *Do you think you have any blind spots?*

TH I don't know. I may be too eclectic sometimes. There's a lot going on with manipulated photography, and so many of the people I really respect have no time at all for it, but I tend to go out of my way to look at material that causes problems for me. I may revere Walker Evans and Lee Friedlander, but at the same time turn around and enter with full enthusiasm into, let's say, Linda Gammel's work. It's a kind of systematic schizophrenia or something, but it's fun.

FG *I think that your method is in part a refusal to allow your personal taste to be the only determinant of your ideas about what the practice of photography is. That's somewhat different from John Szarkowski's exercise of his position as director of photography at The Museum of Modern Art. I think he has a very clear idea of what the practice of photography is. He is much more open and flexible than many people give him credit*

Paul Outerbridge, Jr., *8 O'Clock Coffee: Grinding at the Market*, 1940. Color carbo print

for, but his point of view has limitations, which he would be the first to admit, I think. You seem to feel that your responsibility as curator is to be in some ways as malleable as possible, and that your main criteria for a work's success or failure should be based on what you judge to be the photograph's internal consistency, the appropriateness of means to ends.

TH That's right. That's what I am trying to do.

FG *On the other hand, John Szarkowski has really been a mentor for you, hasn't he?*

TH Without question. I admire enormously what he's done. I don't mean to sound like a mindless acolyte or disciple, but the things that he's written, the exhibitions that he's organized, clearly form a body of work—an accomplishment.

FG *He probably has the most powerfully articulated, clearly argued, persuasively presented theory of the medium to date.*

TH That theory, the way it's worked itself into American photography, is very important to my understanding of photography, as it is for most of us, I think.

FG *A whole host of people out there are angry about that.*

TH But there is no arguing with the significance of what happens at The Museum of Modern Art and the impact that it has.

FG *Do you think that your program has a similar force in this community?*

TH Yes, for good or ill. I'm sure that there are individuals whose work has neither entered the collection nor been exhibited here who feel that there is a certain authoritarianism, unfairness, or lack of responsiveness to work that falls outside a vague set of standards. That's true, but I must necessarily select, edit, respond to, and provide a showcase for the work that I feel is strongest. I couldn't justify seeing the galleries at the museum simply providing a forum for the display of work without strong editorial guidance. It's not just some free-for-all. The Minnesota Artist Exhibition Program, which is meant to be very democratic, has a review panel that can be very severe, in some ways maybe even more severe than a single curator would be. In the beginning, I wasn't quite so trapped by the bureaucracy of the institution. I could put up exhibitions that I hadn't even thought of two weeks previously. Now I'm like everybody else, locked into an exhibition-planning procedure that has us looking seriously at the exhibitions for 1985 and 1986. That's nuts. I'm very envious of small programs, which can plan their shows from one month to the next. I'm jealous of the capacity to be responsive, especially to younger work. Somebody will come in with work that is so exciting, and the next thing you know it's on the walls. In the same vein, I'd also like to be able to have a permanent collection exhibition, much like the photography galleries at The Museum of Modern Art.

FG *Do you think there's anything intentional about the way the bureaucracy of the museum, the planning procedures, all of that business talk and business orientation suppresses the ability of the curators to respond to the freshest things?*

TH Well, it's not in the nature of an institution like ours to be responsive in an immediate and direct way. Planning makes things more manageable for the managers, the people who have to raise the money. They need to know what it is that they're selling. What's the product? What is it that we're trying to fund? They need projections so they can see the pattern. So it is not in their psychology to take the kinds of risks that I as a curator might be perfectly willing to take. They have to be able to pay the electricity bill and make sure that the endowment funds are replenished, and that long-range plans are projected against realistic goals and objectives. That's not typically the way artists operate, so there's a real tension. The businesslike approach to things tends to have a calming effect on the otherwise clamorous and energetic activities of the curators.

FG *Which in turn proceed with more deliberation than the clamorous activities of the artists. So there is a sort of filtering process at work. Do you think, then, that you would have trouble getting overtly political work past the exhibitions committee? Let's say someone made a set of very detailed photographs of victims, not necessarily of wounds and that kind of pornography, but photographs of victims of cluster bombs in Lebanon, and that as part of the presentation the photographer insisted on having a statement that Honeywell had made these cluster bombs in Minneapolis. What would happen?*

TH I think I could convince the committee if I could defend the work on its artistic merits, if I could say this photographer has a vision, has intelligence. If the photographs were successful, the artistic vision would be inseparable from the content. Eugene Richards comes to mind. He's done some really extraordinary pictures, tough and uncompromising. What really affected me about his first book, *Few Comforts or Surprises*

[MIT Press, 1973], was that I was convinced for a long time that he was black, because his pictures of black communities in the Arkansas delta rang so true. He engaged his subjects in a way that was so authentic I couldn't believe that any outsider could have entered into the life his photographs depict. I think that his work can clearly be defended as being so powerfully phrased that it overrides any objections to the content.

Who else comes to mind? Years ago, Danny Seymour had an exhibition, in what was then the hallway just outside my office, of photographs he had taken at the Chicago Democratic Convention. They were an indictment of a political system that had collapsed, and anybody who chose to look could see that. I suspect that the people who would have been offended by the political message didn't really understand what it was they were seeing.

FG *Do you think they would have been more likely to see, to understand, to pick up on that inflection if the pictures had not been in an art museum?*

TH If they had been in a book?

FG *In a book with a suitable verbal content or in a union hall or at the student union of the University of Minnesota. Back to*

Joel D. Levinson, *Fractions*, from the *Self-Indulgence* series, 1979

the question I asked a minute ago: could you really exhibit intensely political work, work that strongly indicted some powerful element in this community, and bring it so close to home?

TH Well, W. Eugene Smith's pictures, which indict big business for irresponsible pollution, for example, are available in exhibition form. The International Center of Photography in New York has that material, and I could borrow it.

FG *But people could dismiss it by saying, "That happened in Japan. We have pollution laws here." But say you had a series of photographs that very explicitly documented persistent violations of Nuclear Regulatory Commission rules at the Prairie Island power plant, with a text that said the odds on this behavior producing a major nuclear accident in the next ten years are twenty to one—in other words, "It's not just those people over there, it's right here"—could you get this exhibition on the walls?*

TH If it was a responsible attempt to deal with the artist's moral responsibility to society, and if, in its realization, it was so compelling that it needed to be seen—if I could feel confident that it was as good as anything else that I could put on those walls, then I would feel obliged to present the work to the exhibitions committee. I would argue as eloquently and as vociferously as I could for the importance of that work's being seen, citing its cogency, its morality, and its artistic integrity. But, right off hand, I don't know a body of work like that. I imagine I could go out and find one, and fashion a show that would deal with those issues. Come to think of it, it's a pretty intriguing idea.

FG *I think one problem, at least in terms of its acceptance by a group of museum professionals, is that this kind of work most likely would not look like Art with a capital* A.

TH That's true. But then there are a lot of things that we consider important in photography that don't look like Art with a big *A*. But you can view a lot of new-generation artists as being highly political. I think you can see Cindy Sherman as being political in a rather interesting way—and Laurie Anderson. I think a lot of rock-and-roll music is highly political, and there is a visual photographic counterpart to a lot that's happening in rock-and-roll music.

FG *You want to do a show of punk photography?*

TH I'm thinking about it. I really am. I think there's a lot of vitality there. A lot of music people are absolute image junkies, and plumbing the depths of that interest, finding out what it is—that's more challenging than anything else I can think of. Maybe it's because it's so mysterious and unknown to me.

There is also the question of what the museum means to the artist. I'm always mindful of the effect that institutional sanction or attention has on an artist, and how that results in a certain self-consciousness, the danger of a certain accommodation. I think that this danger is one of the biggest challenges to an artist in this day and age, when publishing and exhibiting has such a premium placed on it. In advance of that kind of attention or endorsement I think it's totally wrongheaded for artists to sneer at or be disparaging of success, and instead choose to keep their work obscure.

FG *Do you* know *people like that?*

TH You hear artists talk like that all the time: "I don't want to show. It's all so false. That's all establishment crap. I'm not going to play that game. I know my work is good. I don't need to show it. I don't need the validation of that damn gallery. Screw them." But the real challenge is to get in there and swim around and face those sharks and barracudas.

Because of my feeling for the picture maker I am profoundly interested in what you and Friedlander and Harry Callahan and Robert Adams and Robert Heinecken and other successful photographers think about what the museums are doing.

FG *Probably if Film in the Cities [an independent center for film, photography, video, and sound in St. Paul, Minnesota]*

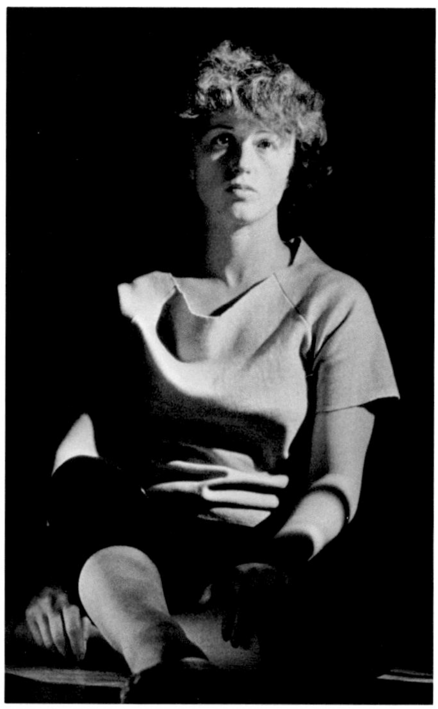

Cindy Sherman, *Untitled*, 1982. Color photograph

and its exhibition program didn't exist, I would feel a lot more dissatisfaction with the availability of current work elsewhere in this community.

TH Well, I think I would be doing exhibitions very differently if it wasn't for Film in the Cities. It's kind of a division of labors, with every arts organization doing its share.

FG *I guess I don't really depend on institutions that much. I would certainly feel a great sense of deprivation if I didn't know that I could drive across town and see prints Walker Evans had made, or all those wonderful images stacked against your cabinets. But somehow, at this point, knowing that the work is there is really quite enough. I think you do a great job, but institutions do what they do. We can't expect them to do everything. And, though I have been asking a lot of questions about it, I'm not even sure an art museum is necessarily the best place to carry out the consequences of political thinking.*

TH Maybe it's a different kind of politics. In 1970 we put up an exhibition of Richard Avedon's photographs, his first major one-person show. I know Avedon's name is apt to arouse an instant reaction from many quarters. I remember in Boston one night in 1969 someone mentioned that I was working on an Avedon show and suddenly every photographer in the room was attacking me: "How dare I?! How dare I consider an exhibition of that work?" That's another issue altogether. But I think that exhibition was particularly important and symbolic for our museum—for me—because it brought to the attention of the public at large a selection of photographs that had been seen and evaluated in completely different terms. Most of the work in that exhibition had been published in books, but it had a far different kind of eloquence and power in this new setting, this new form. It was really extraordinary. And if ever there was an exhibition of great political impact at a museum, it was that one. I remember the night of the opening. The place was just swarming with people; half of them I'd never seen in the museum before—and never saw again, for that matter. In the last gallery, which contained the double-life-size portraits of the Chicago conspirators, it was very crowded, and suddenly one of the people there, a woman who had at one time sung opera, started singing "God Bless America." And everybody started singing "God Bless America" in unison. It was electrifying. I thought the building was going to cave in. It was positively galvanizing to realize that pictures had such power that they could move a whole gallery full of people to that expression of sentiment.

As for my role as a curator, I hope that I understand some of the ways in which work by emerging photographers can enter a museum in an orderly and considered way that is fair to the history of photography—the abiding values we hold—but also allows for the work to be seen in as unfettered a way as possible, without the constraints of the predispositions of a curator, so that the originality of the photographer comes through.

FG *In a way, photography's place in museums is a sign of its coming of age, maybe not the best one we could wish for, but certainly a coming of age in the modernist, self-conscious sense. Perhaps that's something to be desired, perhaps not. Ironically, the closing of galleries recently has meant a breakdown in the system by which new work is disseminated, just at the time when we most need those systems to be functioning well.*

TH I wonder if the breakdown in systems is partly due to a loss of confidence in our ability to respond and give visibility to the work we are affected by, or think is important. Maybe we think it has to be too much of a known quantity before we allow it. I think we are getting too cautious.

FG *That may be part of it. But it's also because the volume of photographs produced is increasing at an extraordinary rate. Photography tried to model itself on painting and sculpture, setting up a commercial gallery system and finding a place in museums, choosing those traditional means to make its vitality and its range of activity known to the public. But the recent acceptance of photography into the museum and gallery world has made us aware of the inherent limitations and distortions of that context. I think we have entered into a healthy period of reevaluation.*

Stephen Scheer: America's Backyard

These photographs were made during the summer of 1980 in a small residential community outside Shelton, Connecticut. The name of the community is The Maples, and it covers a stretch of land about one mile long on the banks of the Housatonic River.

The residents have always liked to think of themselves as river people, and my intention was to document their style of life through color photography.

Summertime seemed to bring out the most of what could be seen at The Maples. The people reunited with the natural surroundings, and their activity was refreshingly uninhibited and festive. I was particularly drawn to the way people adorned themselves and their surroundings, according to their age group and generation.

CL·8936

Rhondal McKinney: Midwestern Moods

I have always worked in or near the classical tradition of documentarians, using the camera in more or less straightforward ways. My background is small town, midwestern and Calvinist enough that I tend to stifle my impulses. Things have their limits. An unfettered intuition is crucial to the research of ideas, but intuition roams most freely over familiar territories.

The earliest of these pictures was made in 1979. Most were made during the past twelve months. All of the photographs were made using the same camera and lens, the same printing methods. Scale, distance, compositional devices vary little from picture to picture. They are held as constants, so to speak. I was originally trained as a scientist, and, although nowadays I research fictions instead of facts, I continue to work in my old style. The documentarian stylist strives for anonymity of voice and discipline of method—devices he uses to make his fictions convincing. No voice is really anonymous, and the artist knows that intelligence comes to his work, if at all, by its own devious ways, quite regardless of a stylized discipline.

My interest in landscape has nothing to do with the conservationist or agriculturist or geologist. The photograph is the important thing to me. I want these photographs to be about the private experience of the individual with the landscape, with the messages it conveys about beauty, nurture, geologic time, and spirituality. Rather than make representations of the land, I want to make photographs that provide a source of direct experience with landscape.

Susan Barron: Beyond Collage

To make space—tear paper.

Cover up in order to reveal.

Secrets unfold as layers are

Pasted—one atop the other. *Sticky*

Press Echo Falling Gone.

These collage/drawings were made between 1979 and 1982.

Michael Spano: City Rhythms

Right: *Spring Street Park*, 1982
Below: *The Saints*, 1982

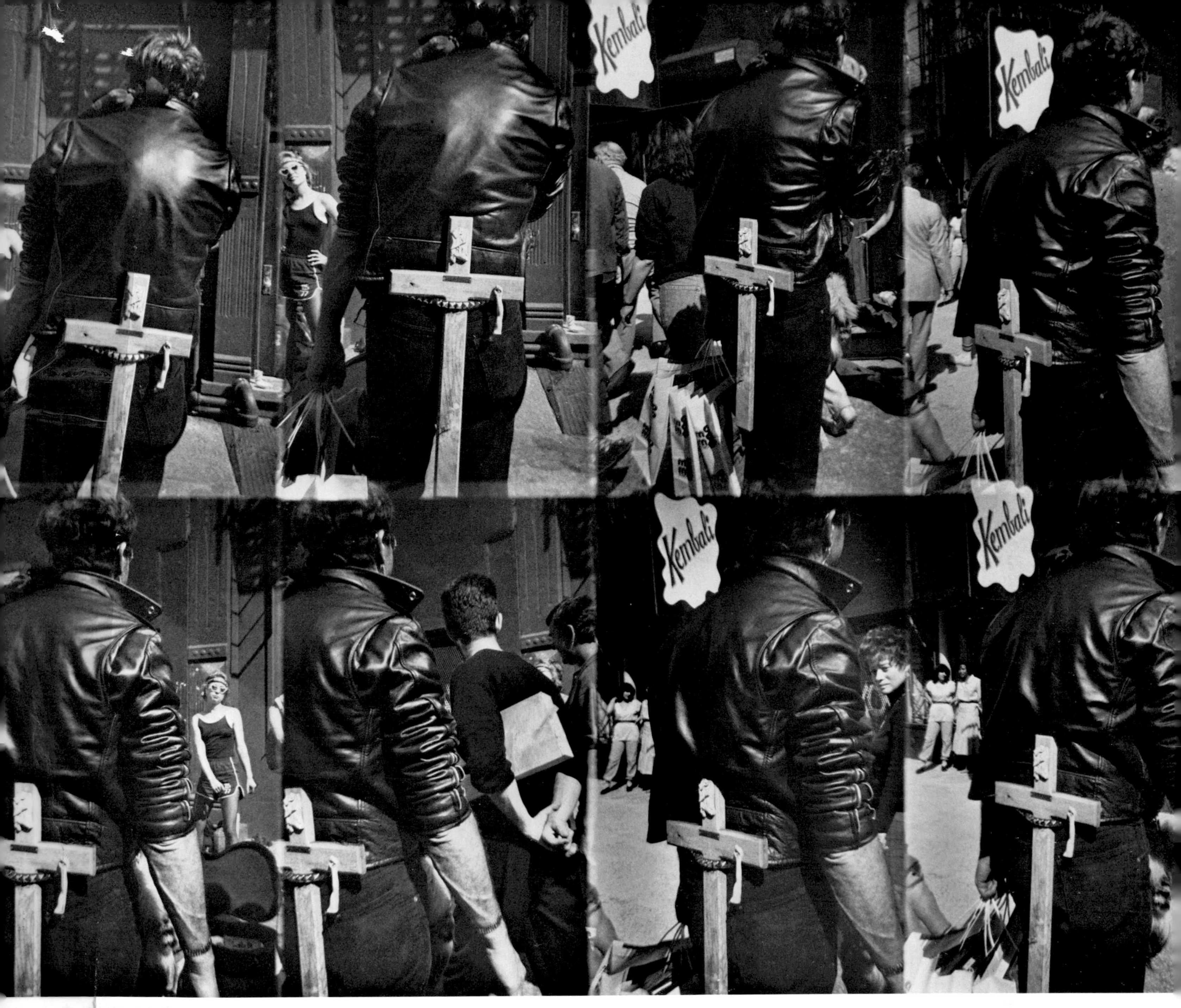

Both: *Untitled*, 1982

The Widelux is a true 35-mm. hand-held panoramic camera because the film is exposed on a curved plane as the lens spans 140 degrees.

My Widelux photographs are urban panoramas. Urban photography entails the ability to participate in the natural rhythms of city life, a domain that is simultaneously public and private. In order to arrange a cultural phenomenon into a picture, I enter small groups of people and establish an intimacy with them, giving me time and space to orchestrate the formal requirements of such a wide-angle picture.

The Graph-Check sequence camera is a 4 x 5-inch box with eight lenses, all shutters fixed at one-thousandth of a second, all apertures set at f/16. The time lapse for all lenses to complete the sequence ranges from a minimum of eight thousandths of a second to a maximum of twenty seconds.

My sequence work is in the twenty-four-second range: every three seconds from the moment I press the shutter release another lens takes another picture until all eight lenses expose a different section of film.

My Widelux and sequence work both deal with what I call the "durational" mode of photography: the photograph represents a time interval longer than one instantaneous moment.

Street Scene, 1981

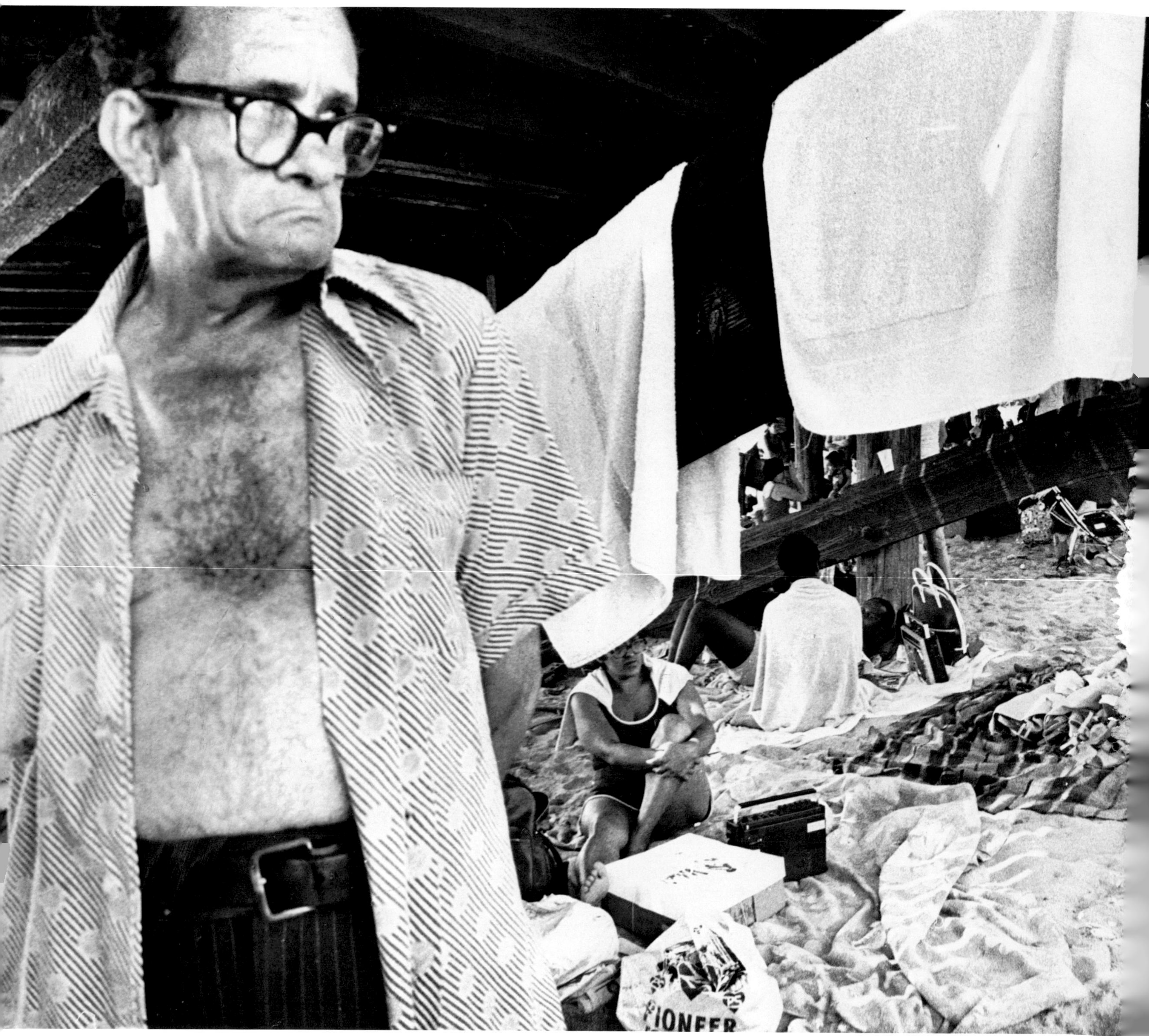

Coney Island, from the *Under the Boardwalk* series, 1980

Southampton, 1981

Photography: Tradition and Decline

By Carol Squiers

The radiant promise of the latest photography boom has shriveled and all but disappeared. Once again the market for art photography has proven to be unstable and short-lived, as it has in the past. The European Pictorialists, for example, had begun to chip out a niche for themselves in the nineteenth-century salons, when incipient public support and sales evaporated. In 1933 Ansel Adams launched a milder attempt to sell the wares of the Group f/64 in a gallery open to the public, only to have the gallery fail a few years later. Even Beaumont Newhall, as curator of The Museum of Modern Art's new photography department in the 1940s, tried to encourage photography collecting by offering original prints by such masters as Alfred Stieglitz and Edward Weston for ten dollars apiece. Now photography galleries around the country have closed, and of the two seemingly durable creators of the boom, Light Gallery in New York City is virtually out of business, and Harry Lunn in Washington, D.C., will operate only as a private dealer. Other galleries that exhibited photography along with painting and sculpture have hastily reorganized, reducing their commitment to photography. Most conspicuous among them is New York's Castelli Graphics, where a once separate photography department was absorbed as a subdepartment after as many as one-half its photographers had been released. Other photography galleries, such as Daniel Wolf in New York, have diversified and have begun showing more readily salable items such as ethnic masks and Indian rugs. Why has this disconcerting collapse occurred after less than a decade of prosperity? The economy, we know, is in terrible shape. But despite some shaky periods, the rest of the art market has been able to survive. Why hasn't the photography market done the same?

The entrepreneurial aspects of the boom are another article, but they must be mentioned. The broad outlines of the situation include undercapitalization and the overextension of finances. (Light Gallery in particular may have spread itself too thin by trying to expand its New York gallery and by opening a Los Angeles branch.) In addition, dealers offered discount packages, selling groups of prints at radically reduced rates to collectors and groups of investors, netting large single payments while undermining the market as a whole. And, finally, it is evident that many of the new collectors who appeared overnight were either naïve dilettantes or uninterested investors out for a fast killing in a new market. Many of both types have disappeared, taking the boom with them.

Aside from financial manipulations and unwise business practices, there may be other reasons for the recent debacle. The suddenness and completeness of photography's collapse suggests the entire superstructure of the boom may have been built on an armature of pictures too weak to withstand the pressures of either intelligent scrutiny or the marketplace. As the seventies wore on, an aura of banality and redundancy began to permeate photography exhibitions.

The history of twentieth-century photography began inauspiciously. The retrograde style of Pictorialism, born of photography's defensiveness about its status as art, exemplified a problem that has plagued photography ever since. Modern art photography has spent much of its time looking back over its shoulder, either at the example of painting or at its own short history. Instead of inventing a future, it has woven itself into the past, recapitulating the details of its official family tree again and again in a desperate attempt to fabricate a respectable tradition for itself. As a result, instead of fulfilling a promise for innovation, photography became trapped in its own deadening system of academies.

The one realm of culture in which photography has played a decidedly formative role—commercial photography in all of its various manifestations—has been treated as an unsavory colony that occasionally produces worthy talents like Weegee or Richard Avedon. Because of its piecemeal, masterpiece orientation adopted from the history of art, photographic history has been both unwilling and unable to deal with the visual systems of magazines and newspapers, which have illustrated and helped define how modern civilization looks. By isolating single, out-of-context examples of news, advertising, or fashion photography and treating them only as objects of documentary or aesthetic interest, photography has amputated a good part of its own living body. Instead, as late as 1981, in the exhibition *Before Photography,* The Museum of Modern Art tacked up forgettable oil sketches and paintings in order to validate photography's supposed fine art parentage.

Originally, the theory goes, photography took representation away from painting, so painting became modernist,

meaning formalist, meaning involved with its own qualities and capabilities.
Andy Grundberg, *Soho Weekly News,* April 26, 1979

Modernist art practice was built on the bedrock of radical challenge. It defied traditional definitions of subject matter and pictorial construction and in the process questioned a whole range of cultural assumptions, from the value of art as a contemplative experience to the primacy of the rational mind, to the assumed superiority of Western civilized culture in general. At its most rarefied it proposed that art be freed from all but its own self-referential considerations. It was this latter, narrower definition that modernist photography fixed upon and which remained its most heralded attribute.

When Paul Strand wrote in 1917 of the need to recognize photography's "complete uniqueness of means" and condemned the handwork of the Pictorialists, he unknowingly provided the seeds of a new dogma of technique to replace the old. Although he named "intensity of vision" and "the photographer's point of view toward Life" as important, they were vague abstractions in comparison to the more attainable goal of fulfilling photography's special calling through such means as the expression of the subject "through a range of almost infinite tonal values." In this same signal piece of writing Strand made another point that has informed photographic modernism to the present day. He extolled the very tradition he implicitly castigated in his work, paying homage to Stieglitz and selected Pictorialists. This desire to remain bound to tradition, along with the idea of the self-referential, communicative power of photography's "special" means, echoed down over the next seventy years.

If we do keep faith with our vision, we will be equally able to protect old photographic traditions against senseless onslaughts and see to it that new imagery and styles of younger artists are not recklessly destroyed.
Henry Holmes Smith, "Three Photographers," 1961

New pictures derive first of all from old pictures. What an artist brings to his work that is new—special to his own life and his own eyes—is used to challenge and revise his tradition, as he knows it.
John Szarkowski, *New Photography USA,* 1971

Our exhibitions explore the future directions of photography in the context of historical precedent.
Charles Traub, *Light Catalogue,* 1981

It was the Group f/64, in particular Edward Weston and Ansel Adams, who in the 1930s and 1940s first produced a complete body of work proclaiming the doctrine of photography's intrinsic properties. Their scrupulous attention to the subtleties of exposure, the delineation of detail and tonality, and the general virtues of the fine print made Weston, Adams, and the other "straight" photographers models to be followed for decades. But Weston made a prophetic error of interpretation when, in order to support his belief in the communicative resonance of photographic means, he quoted William Blake: "Man is led to believe a lie, when he sees with, not through the eye." Weston went on to say that the camera could do what Blake wanted, it could "enable one to see through the eye, augmenting the eye, seeing more than the eye sees, exaggerating details, recording surfaces, textures" ("Photography—Not Pictorial," *Camera Craft,* 1930). Weston transformed the mystical penetration alluded to in Blake's line into a function of the camera's superior powers of "seeing," a belief that inspired all subsequent modes of photographic formalism. And, as Margery Mann pointed out, this once revolutionary position did indeed become the base for a "new establishment," especially on the West Coast, for the next thirty years (*Imogen,* 1974, p. 14). With the publication of Adams's books on technique in the 1940s and 1950s the tradition of modern photography was firmly established with a set of readily available texts to disseminate it.

Except for the pedagogical substrata provided by the program at the Institute of Design in Chicago, the next significant public contribution to official photographic canons occurred in John Szarkowski's book *The Photographer's Eye* (1965). Szarkowski firmly anchored himself in the lineage of photographic modernism by defining his five categories of photographic concerns as "section views through the body of photographic tradition." Two statements within this text are particularly important for an understanding of much of the art photography that was recognized in the 1960s and 1970s:

He [the photographer] could not, outside the studio, pose the truth; he could only record it as he found it, and it was found in nature in a fragmented and unexplained form—not as a story, but as scattered and suggestive clues. The photographer could not assemble these clues into a coherent narrative, he could only isolate the fragment, document it, and by so doing claim for it some special significance. . . .

The phrase the decisive moment . . . *has been misunderstood; the thing that happens at the decisive moment is not a dramatic climax but a visual one. The result is not a story but a picture.*
John Szarkowski, *The Photographer's Eye,* 1965

In these statements Szarkowski defines the photographer's role as an essentially mysterious pursuit of trivial incident and detail that will somehow rise to the status of "symbols." By denying any narrative possibility for photographs, he rejected *narrative*'s shared root with *knowing.* When the photographer ventured out to face the "unexplained" clues in the outside world, which *could not* be assembled into a coherent narrative, he was to do so with a blank mind. Beauty was to be found in the photographer's ability to order the flux of time, although this had "little to do with what was happening." Thus, the art photographer was freed both from prior thought and from the responsibility to interpret what was in front of him. His only goal was to arrange a disconnected, meaningless world into beautiful but purely visual compositions. The photographer was never to attempt articulation of meaning—before, during, or after the moment he released the shutter. Art photography

James Henkel, *Monogram Guest Towel*, 1978

had at last produced a text that explained how Weston's "vital essences" could be discovered in anything, provided the pictures were well made. The pursuit of unknown and unknowable fragments, constructed by the self-reflexive rules of the newly expanded tradition of modernist photography, thus received official sanction.

> *The 1979–80 gallery season lacked much of the vigor, the newness, that characterized photography since its "discovery" in the early 1970s.*
>
> Andy Grundberg, *Soho Weekly News*, September 10, 1980

> *I had to face the truth: I was bored stiff by art photography.*
>
> Shelley Rice, *Soho Weekly News*, October 12, 1978

The photographic gallery system that sprang up in the 1970s had already begun to seem spent and lifeless before the end of the decade. Light Gallery, along with The Museum of Modern Art, was the premier showcase for twentieth-century photography. Light showed older masters, such as Ansel Adams, Harry Callahan, and Aaron Siskind, and younger photographers who produced variations on established genres, such as Garry Winogrand, Michael Bishop, Emmet Gowin, and Stephen Shore. In addition, Light represented a phalanx of experimental "idea" photographers whose work derived almost entirely from art world examples of painting, printmaking, and conceptual art, such as Robert Heinecken, Carl Toth, Thomas Barrow, and Keith Smith. Michael Bishop's work and career provide a good example (of the many that could be discussed) of how photographic modernism's lineage finally showed its undeniable exhaustion.

Bishop's entire pursuit has been to demonstrate the way camera vision can produce an odd or nonsensical ordering of objects in space. His subject matter consists of flat or simple forms—street signs, fences, call boxes, park benches. Using a perspectival control lens, he lines up objects in the frame to create odd juxtapositions, flattening space and making some objects appear to be connected or to have some relation to one another. He extrapolated this theme in both black-and-white and color photographs and had five one-person shows of the work at Light between 1973 and 1978.

Like much contemporary photography, Bishop's work is a minute fragment lifted from the "tradition" of photography

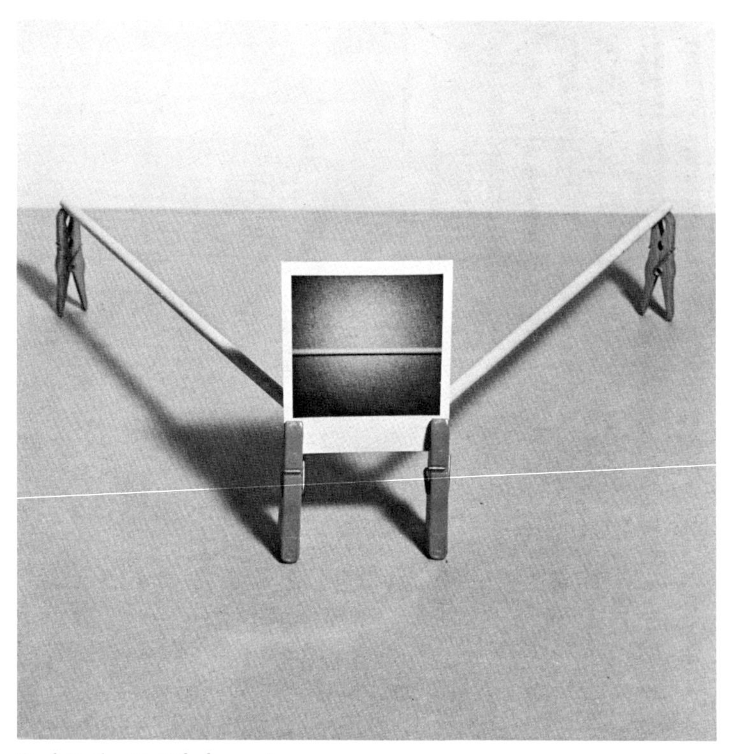

Carl Toth, *Untitled*, 1978

and inflated many times out of proportion to its interest. Its progenitor is a single picture of Walker Evans, of a telephone pole and painted signs, *Gas Station, Reedsville, West Virginia*, 1936. In the late 1960s and early 1970s Lee Friedlander expanded on the themes of perspectival collapse and peculiarly modern visual confusion, and energized the ideas with his particular brand of intelligent wit. When Bishop stretched this segment of an idea into a career, he did it solely in formal terms, tidying up Friedlander's rough edges with the niceties of technique—toned black-and-white prints, flash, and "altered" color printing. What had originally been an expressive and documentary subject—the conjunction of disparate cultural signs—had been emptied of content and used as a vehicle for bravura technique.

Bishop was not alone in his vision of the camera's art. Along with the notion of a heightened self-reflexivity came the fully accepted doctrine of "nominal subject matter." The phrase, which appeared repeatedly in photographic writing of the 1970s, is used to indicate that the subject matter is secondary to the photographic treatment. In considering the bad reviews that greeted Robert Frank's *The Americans* when it was first published in 1958, John Szarkowski wrote: "It was in other words not the nominal subject matter of Frank's work that shocked the photography audience but the pictures themselves, the true content of which cannot be described in terms of iconography, since it also concerns a new method of photographic description" (*Mirrors and Windows,* 1978, p. 20). Although he had just quoted pointedly negative responses to the

Michael Bishop, *Untitled,* 1977(?)

"iconography," Szarkowski still chose to emphasize Frank's stylistic revolt instead of acknowledging that Frank's revolutionary (for art photography) critical approach to subject matter had at least equal importance. Although such misguided praise can never ultimately detract from the impact of Frank's pictures, Szarkowski's interpretation sums up a position that has institutionalized the emptiness of much contemporary photography. An artist like Michael Bishop has had implicit official support for his choice of subject matter, which looks "serious" (ubiquitous functional industrial artifacts) but is really just a skeleton on which to hang increasingly refined technique.

A similar fascination with technique and a rebellion against its conservative canons lie at the heart of so-called experimental and conceptual photography. To tear up, write on, paste on, or otherwise alter the surface of a photograph, or to make that surface out of any one of a number of nonsilver "avant-garde" processes, was once, and in some circles still is, considered to be a hallmark of advanced photographic practice. The violation of the exquisitely detailed surface that Weston thought emanated his vital new way of seeing continued through the 1960s to be an accepted act of defiance, and in the 1970s was enshrined in the gallery and museum.

Robert Heinecken is one of the most influential practitioners of this mode. His achievement has been to give the appearance of daring both in choice of subject—naked women—and in handling—collaged imagery, painted-on emulsion, and hand

Robert Heinecken, *Cliché Vary / Autoeroticism,* 1974

coloring with chalk on canvas, among others. He reproduced pornographic imagery for a middle-class gallery audience, which in that context could be taken as critical commentary while it reaped the benefits of titillating, aestheticized display. Thus he could capitalize on the stimulation value while appearing to perform the revolutionary actions of bringing forbidden subject matter into the gallery and challenging the conventions of good photography at the same time. (But what could be more common, in art or commercial photography, than naked women?) The "liberating" example of Heinecken's procedures has provided a model for more elementary kinds of rebellion. James Henkel, for instance, could comfortably scribble an alphabet on a color picture of a towel. For such embarrassingly childish maneuvers he was rewarded with two one-person shows at Light, a museum exhibition in Minneapolis, and a grant from the National Endowment for the Arts.

Ultimately it is the support system of photography—the museums (especially The Museum of Modern Art), galleries, educational institutions, granting process, books, magazines, and the critics who write about photographic events—that is responsible for nourishing and applauding the meager achievements of photography over the last ten years. The photographic establishment made it clear that any ambitious photographer had to learn the lessons of the masters and in effect become a practitioner of a recognizable style in one academy or another in order to be considered serious. Photography's favorite critics have been expected to buttress and encourage photography, rather than to examine it rigorously. Although they were not critical writings, John Szarkowski's intelligent and eloquent texts have to a certain extent provided a standard and have consequently been frozen into holy writ. Critical articles that have called photography's bluff—by A. D. Coleman, Douglas Crimp, Craig Owens, and Abigail Solomon-Godeau, for example—have been dismissed or simply ignored. Szarkowski pinpointed a major demand of the photography audience when he noted that to Robert Frank's critics it seemed that Frank lacked the proper "affection" for the medium. An uncritical reverence for the medium has immensely damaged its capacity to grow.

The Institute of Design in Chicago was until recently the most important wellspring of photographic education. Although it is in part responsible for the increasing formalism in photography, it promoted one principle that remains central to the nature of photography. László Moholy-Nagy and Harry Callahan taught that ideas in photography were best realized in an extended series of pictures. But they did not bargain on the power of the museum and the marketplace. By defining the nature of photography as the recording of isolated and ultimately inexplicable but symbolic fragments, Szarkowski helped splinter the integrity of the series. If each photograph was considered as a self-contained "symbol" in its own right, instead of a building block in a larger pattern, then a single instant could always stand for the whole. This theory served the museum well because even though one-person exhibitions contained a range of a photographer's work, only one or two examples could ultimately be absorbed by the system once the temporary show came down from the walls. Pictures that functioned best in the context of a series could not function in a situation where isolated representative examples of excellence were needed. The idea served the gallery system too, since the gallery needs single, self-contained works to sell to its customers.

By exalting the primacy of wholly private expression, art photography has ignored several important issues crucial to cultural assessment of photography as a medium. Unlike the other arts, which the public has always seen as special, otherworldly activities, photography is part of the everyday experience of most people. Popular response to photographs is conditioned by public as well as private use, and the public role of photographs cannot be ignored. The formulaic, massive, and highly effective methods of invoking social fears and private desires developed by the mass media have provided the major training ground for photographic understanding. As Christopher Phillips reveals in a recent article ("The Judgment Seat of Photography," *October*, Fall 1982), the museum felt the reverberations of mass opinion within its very walls. Beaumont Newhall initiated the fine art photography exhibition program at The Museum of Modern Art in 1940, but it had little impact. When his successor, Edward Steichen, began mounting exhibitions based on the narrative techniques of picture magazines—most notably *The Family of Man* in 1955—the public began turning out in droves and critics responded enthusiastically. Although one could dismiss this phenomenon as evidence of the mindless low-brow ardor for second-rate culture, to do so would be a mistake. Artists must begin to come to terms with the pervasive, multiple uses of photography and especially with its impact through the media. In its anxiety to shed its identity as the stepchild of painting, art photography isolated itself in the name of modernism, no longer mimicking other art forms but opting for a narrow definition that quickly became sterile rather than nourishing. For the sake of its future survival, photography must establish communication with other art forms, as well as with the entire public arena of photography.

People and Ideas

(continued from page 3)

neither great nor proud; it is best described as twisted, and he has imposed that vision with all his editorial might on his new book, *Bearing Witness.* This too is a book made by someone from someone else's photographs, only in this case Lesy has made a profession of the process. Beginning with his Rutgers University thesis, published as *Wisconsin Death Trip* in 1973, he has produced four thematic books, using photographs to support the theme. *Bearing Witness* is Lesy's selection of pictures from the immense photography collections of the Library of Congress, the National Archives, and the Pentagon.

Lesy has a fine eye for selecting photographs, and he can write well. He seems to look up to photographers, perhaps because he uses their pictures, and writes some romantic things about how the photographer works. But for all his admiration of them, he does not bother to place a credit line with their photographs. His most interesting writing is about the collections themselves, and in particular about the work of Paul Vanderbilt in creating them. But he has also written a lot of impenetrable junk laced with names like Jung, Goethe, and that of a medieval book maker he admires, although some of the books Lesy copies were printed much more recently.

By the second page of Lesy's text I began to suspect he was nuts. By the third page Lesy writes that he did go a little nuts looking through all those photographs, and that might explain the rest of the book. *Bearing Witness* claims to be a photographic chronicle of American life from the years 1860 to 1945. It is not. It is a tremendous manipulation of photographs, often great photographs, beautifully reproduced, to create a piece of photoliterature. It is Michael Lesy's version of the American past, using photographs. But for me the work fails. I am offended by Lesy's vision and his use of other people's photographs to achieve it.

Lesy presents an America that gets grimmer and grimmer as the book progresses. It is mostly involved in wars. In fact about half his selections are about war, and it ends with pictures of European concentration camp survivors and Senator Barkley from Kentucky staring at a pile of corpses at Buchenwald. Since it is not mentioned in the text, I would like to point out that Americans did not build Buchenwald, we liberated it. The back of the book calls Mr. Lesy a "photographer/historian." What makes a historian think that practically half the history of this country can be presented in a single volume containing a few hundred photographs?

Anonymous, *Senator Alben W. Barkley of Kentucky, Buchenwald, Germany,* April 1945

I do not really object to Lesy's trying to create a book of vision, manipulating photographs, or even using other people's photographs. I object to his vision itself. It is much too private, and much too depressing to be presented as "a chronicle of American life." I also happen to think it is inaccurate. Attacking the American past in 1982 is about as appropriate as kicking the dead bodies in the Buchenwald photograph. What is the point? A decade or two ago there was a purpose in bringing low the American image. Today, if there is any purpose, it is the opposite. It is a time to feel good about our lives, for that is all that we have.

There is another way to look at Mr. Lesy's book. Skip the preface and the introduction by Lesy and look through the pictures as if they were a movie. Born from the Civil War, the work begins with a stunning landscape of soldiers and a grave at Antietam. The Indian camp at Deadwood and the Manhattan Bridge under construction are overwhelming pictures with which Lesy begins two of his chapters. We are, with photographs like these, racing through America, through incredible times, and growth and democratic glory. The tremendous variety and beauty of American landscapes and American people is before us. Much of that variety and beauty, of course, is now gone. Opening the section "Misfortunes" is another overpowering landscape of "the Johnstown flood," similar to the picture of Antietam. "Women after the War" opens with a group portrait of no less than a dozen young women who work as rivet passers, seated triumphantly before a navy ship. Taken twenty-four years later is another portrait of a young woman, this time "girl alone at the Sea Grill"—a woman waiting at a bar. Change and the speed of it has probably been the dominant fact of the century. Finally, America fights through World War II, and finds itself, through the figure of Senator Barkley, confronting the horror of the dead at Buchenwald. Not a very nice end to the story, but a kinder way to see Lesy's work.

DANNY LYON

Walker Evans at Work. With an essay by Jerry L. Thompson. 239 pages, 745 photographs. New York: Harper & Row, 1982. $18.95.

Michael Lesy, *Bearing Witness.* 172 pages, 275 photographs. New York: Pantheon Books, 1982. Cloth, $27.50; paper, $15.00.

CONTRIBUTORS

Susan Barron

Susan Barron was trained as a musician and holds an advanced degree in clinical diagnostic chemistry. She was introduced to photography by Art Sinsabaugh in 1969, and her photographs and collages are included in major collections.

Frank Gohlke

Frank Gohlke is best known for his pictures documenting the destruction by tornado of his hometown of Wichita Falls, Texas (*Aperture* 86). His most recent photographs are aerial views of the Oklahoma landscape, and pictures showing the aftermath of the Mount St. Helens eruptions.

Ted Hartwell

Ted Hartwell has been curator of photography at the Minneapolis Institute of Arts since 1963. He was an aerial photographer for the Marine Corps and did commercial work for periodicals and advertising agencies. In 1976 and 1977 Hartwell was project director of the Minnesota Survey, a documentary photographic project.

Nancy Hellebrand

In 1971 Nancy Hellebrand began to study with master portraitist Bill Brandt, after operating from her own commercial studio for four years. Hellebrand is currently associate professor of photography at Bucks County Community College in Pennsylvania.

John Lueders-Booth

In 1970 John Lueders-Booth left his position as an insurance administrator to pursue his interest in photography. He is currently manager of the photography laboratory of the Carpenter Center for the Visual Arts at Harvard University and an instructor of photography. Grants from the National Endowment for the Arts, The Artist's Foundation, Inc., and the Polaroid Corporation helped him complete his Framingham prison project.

Danny Lyon

A photographer for over twenty years, Danny Lyon has most recently published *Pictures from the New World* (Aperture, 1981), a survey of his photographs since 1962.

Rhondal McKinney

Rhondal McKinney has worked as a railroad brakeman, mathematics teacher, and offset printer as well as a commercial photographer and an instructor of photography. He will curate an exhibition of midwestern landscape photography at the Art Institute of Chicago in the summer of 1983.

William Maguire

William Maguire holds a Master's degree in photography from the Institute of Design, Illinois Institute of Technology, and an advanced degree in English. He is currently an associate professor of photography at Florida International University in Miami.

Carter Ratcliff

As a contributing editor of *Saturday Review, Art in America, Art International*, and *Picture*, Carter Ratcliff has written extensively on contemporary art. His books include *Botero* (Abbeville Press, 1980), *Joseph Cornell* (The Museum of Modern Art, 1981), and *Andy Warhol* (Abbeville Press, forthcoming).

Stephen Scheer

Stephen Scheer has published work in commercial magazines since receiving his Master of Fine Arts in photography from Yale University in 1980. He is currently visiting lecturer in photography at Yale. His most recent work-in-progress documents the landscape and people of Quebec and the Gaspé Peninsula.

Michael Spano

Michael Spano is co-director of the Midtown Y Gallery in New York City, and has taught photography at Queens College and at Cooper Union. His work has been published in *The Village Voice* and *New York* magazine.

Carol Squiers

Carol Squiers writes photography criticism for *The Village Voice*, *Artforum*, *Modern Photography*, and *Vogue*. In 1981 she received an Art Critics Fellowship Grant from the National Endowment for the Arts. She has been curator of photography at P. S. 1, the Institute for Art and Urban Resources, in Long Island City, since 1980.

CREDITS

Page 3 photographs from *Walker Evans at Work* copyright © 1982 The Estate of Walker Evans, courtesy Harper & Row. Pages 4, 7 photographs courtesy The Lunn Gallery, Washington, D.C. Page 5 photograph courtesy Abbeville Press (The McCrory Collection, New York). Page 6 photograph from *Edward Weston: His Life and Photographs,* copyright © 1973, 1979 Aperture, Inc. Pages 34, 38 photographs courtesy The Minneapolis Institute of Arts. Page 37 photograph courtesy The Robert Miller Gallery, New York. Page 39 photograph courtesy Metro Pictures, New York. Page 74 photographs from *Light Gallery Catalogue*, copyright © 1981 Light Gallery, New York. Page 75 photograph by Michael Bishop from *Michael Bishop,* copyright © 1979 Chicago Center for Contemporary Photography; photograph by Robert Heinecken from John Szarkowski, *Mirrors and Windows: American Photography Since 1960,* copyright © 1978 The Museum of Modern Art, New York. Page 77 photograph from *Bearing Witness,* copyright © 1982 Michael Lesy, courtesy Pantheon Books (Pentagon, U.S. Army Signal Corps SC 204745). Pages 8–31, 40–62 photographs courtesy the artists.

Cover: Jane Tuckerman, *Untitled,* 1980.

Composition by David E. Seham Assoc., Inc., Metuchen, New Jersey. Black-and-white printing by Meriden Gravure, Inc., Meriden, Connecticut. Contone® color separation and printing by L S Graphic Inc.—D. L. Terwilliger Company, Inc., New York.

Aperture Patrons

Ansel Adams, Carmel, California
Arthur M. Bullowa, New York, New York
Shirley C. Burden, Beverly Hills, California
D. S. and R. H. Gottesman Foundation, New York, New York
John H. Gutfreund, New York, New York
Mr. and Mrs. Peter Haas, Jr., San Francisco, California
Robert A. Hauslohner, Rosemont, Pennsylvania
David McAlpin, Princeton, New Jersey
Robert and Joyce Menschel, New York, New York
National Endowment for the Arts, Washington, D.C.
Irving Rose, Northbrook, Illinois
The San Francisco Foundation
Charles Schaff, Evanston, Illinois
Bernard and Marion Stein Foundation
Estate of Hazel Strand
Estate of Paul Strand
Estate of Minor White

Donors

Jonas Dovydenas, Lenox, Massachusetts
Frederick S. Kullman, New Orleans, Louisiana

Friends

Mrs. Marguerite Rule Johnstone, New York, New York
William P. Steele, New York, New York
Michael Turok, Seattle, Washington
Harry Drake, St. Paul, Minnesota

Sustaining Subscribers

Susan Adams-Marks, Newton, Massachusetts
Joan Almond, Malibu, California
Robert Anthoine, New York, New York
Joan Baron, New York, New York
Gerald Belpaire, New York, New York
Charles T. Bell, Holly Hill, Florida
Tom Benoit, Mill Valley, California
Gay Block, Houston, Texas
Dr. Susan Boiko, Abilene, Texas
Robert A. Brockman, Tucson, Arizona
Robin Bruce, Palo Cedro, California
Dr. and Mrs. Robert Bunnen, Atlanta, Georgia
Dr. Charles J. Burstin, Beverly Hills, California
Edward Carye, East Cambridge, Massachusetts
Daniel R. Childs, New Canaan, Connecticut
Cesar Cordova, Mexico
Richard Crook, Flint, Michigan
James F. Cunningham, Schenectady, New York
Charles Daniels, Whittier, California
Robert Davey, Los Angeles, California
Edward De Stefano, Freehold, New Jersey
David B. Devine, San Francisco, California
Dennis Dilmaghani, Purchase, New York
Richard F. Dixon, Jr., Manasquan, New Jersey
Paul M. Dougan, Salt Lake City, Utah
The Edipa Foundation, New York, New York
Lyle Fain, Providence, Rhode Island
Royal R. Faubion, Chicago, Illinois
David Finn, New York, New York
The Fonda Group, Greenwich, Connecticut
Col. D. Frazier, Augusta, Georgia
James B. Fulton, Kewanee, Illinois
F. Fuste, Miami, Florida
Emanuel Gerard, New York, New York
Alan Gould, Santa Fe, New Mexico
Manfred Heiting, Frankfurt, West Germany
Matthias Hermani, Vancouver, Canada
Candace Beatty Howard, Denver, Colorado
Herb Inglove, Pacific Palisades, California
Frederick L. Jacobs, White Plains, New York
Jennifer Johnson, Jacksonville, Florida
Phyllis and Donald Kahn, Minneapolis, Minnesota
Dr. M. Anwar Kamal, Jacksonville, Florida
Mary A. Knapp, Grand Rapids, Michigan
Eddie Krieger, Abilene, Texas
Thaddeus B. Kubis, Port Washington, New York
William M. Lee, Long Beach, California
David M. Levy, Deal, New Jersey
Richard Lindenberg, Hialeah Gardens, Florida
Rodney J. McKim, San Francisco, California
Donald W. McPhail, Philadelphia, Pennsylvania
A. Mamari, London, England
Barbara Marshall, Chestnut Hill, Massachusetts
Grace M. Mayer, New York, New York
Michael Meagher, Oakville, Canada
Richard S. Menschel, New York, New York
Robert and Joyce Menschel, New York, New York
Harvey S. Shipley Miller, Fort Washington, Pennsylvania
Toomis Mitt, Evanston, Illinois
D. C. Mulcare, New York, New York
Stephen E. Myers, Akron, Ohio
Beaumont Newhall, Santa Fe, New Mexico
Rial Ogden, Washington Depot, Connecticut
Michael S. Osborn, Riverside, California
Dr. and Mrs. Robert Page, Dallas, Texas
William Penn Foundation, Philadelphia, Pennsylvania
Dr. Tom Philbrook, Houston, Texas
G. Neil Phillips, Atlanta, Georgia
Photography by Bordeaux, Portland, Oregon
H. Joseph Plack, Chicago, Illinois
Bernard Rickenbach, Staten Island, New York
Richard Roaman, Roslyn Estates, New York
Richard M. Ross, Columbus, Ohio
Charles Schaff, Jr., Evanston, Illinois
Carlos Hugh Schenck, Minneapolis, Minnesota
John Schlobohm, Malibu, California
Dr. Joan H. Shalack and Dr. Jerome A. Shiell, Pasadena, California
Mitchell W. Shearer, Jr., Marshalltown, Iowa
Paul Smart, Lawrence, Kansas
Robert L. Smith, Hartland, Wisconsin
Anthony P. Spare, Hillsborough, California
Michael G. Stan, Columbus, Ohio
Arthur O. Stein, San Jose, California
Rodney D. Susholtz, Houston, Texas
Pearl Sutter, Washington, D.C.
Robert A. Taub, Dearborn, Michigan
Michael and Elinor Tourtellot, Lecompton, Kansas
Mrs. Thomas I. Unterberg, New York, New York
Miki Warner, Malibu, California
Arnold S. Warwick, New York, New York
David R. Wilson, Rochester, New York
Dr. Dan Zavela, Grosse Pointe Woods, Michigan

Retaining Subscribers

Michael P. Accord, Long Beach, California
Blair Amundsen, Lethridge, Canada
Eduardo Aparicio-Baldo, Evanston, Illinois
Paul Axelrod, New York, New York
Robert Azzi, New York, New York
Jeff Bacon, Houston, Texas
Michael G. Barefoot, Dunn, North Carolina
Robert Barton, Edmonton, Canada
Jacques Baruch Gallery, Chicago, Illinois
John and Jennie Baynard, Auburndale, Massachusetts
Arthur Beaudette, N. Brookfield, Massachusetts
Joe Bein, Los Angeles, California
Arthur Bell, Chicago, Illinois
Jim Bengston, Oslo, Norway
J. D. Beyer, Shrewsbury, New Jersey
Victor Bloomfield, Edina, Minnesota
James Blue, Rockville, Maryland
Charles R. Blyth, Cambridge, Massachusetts
Richard L. Bohanon, Oklahoma City, Oklahoma
Donald M. Bradburn, New Orleans, Louisiana
Stevan H. Brodie, Saudi Arabia
Charles Cannizzaro, Sherman Oaks, California
Jenise M. Cardwell, Little Rock, Arkansas
Henry Chezar, Grand View, New York
Gene Chmura, Lisle, Illinois
Bradford T. Clark, Wayne, Pennsylvania
Robert P. Colborn, Bluffton, South Carolina
Anthony T. Colburn, Arcata, California
Charles D. Collins, Templeton, Massachusetts
D. Jose Ignacio de Velasco Colmenares, Madrid, Spain
Robert James Craig, Miami, Florida
John F. Dalton, Harrisburg, Pennsylvania
C. M. Day, New Canaan, Connecticut
Charles W. Denham, Pittsburgh, Pennsylvania
Kim Despain, Provo, Utah
Woody Deutsch, Decherd, Tennessee
Jouke Dijkstra, Haarlem, Netherlands
Paul H. Doherty, Cheshire, Connecticut
Jay Branch, Rego Park, New York
Patricia Monaco Drew, Oakland, California
Duane Dudley, Des Moines, Iowa
Mac and Eugenie Dupont, Hochessin, Delaware
Michael Eastman Photography, St. Louis, Missouri
Dr. Daniel Edelstone, Pittsburgh, Pennsylvania
John Edstrom, Calgary, Canada
Anne Ehrenkranz, New York, New York
Mrs. George Ehrenkranz, Hollywood, Florida
John R. Eigler, Wayne, Pennsylvania
J. Mitchell Ellis, Glasgow, Kentucky
Bradford M. Endicott, Boston, Massachusetts
Alf L. Erickson, Fort Lauderdale, Florida
Michael Faeder, New York, New York
Joseph Fallon, San Francisco, California
David Feldman, Los Angeles, California
Barry Fellman, Miami, Florida
Scott Ferguson, St. Louis, Missouri
Dr. Julian Hart Fisher, Brookline, Massachusetts
M. Flomen, Montreal, Canada
Michael H. Ford, Los Angeles, California
Phoebe Franklin, Atlanta, Georgia
John Fuller, Paddington, Australia
J. B. Fulton, Kewanee, Illinois
John Robert Fulton, San Jose, California
Robert and Fay Gage, Pound Ridge, New York
Aileen C. Gagney, West Brattleboro, Vermont
James P. Garland, Portland, Maine
Tom Garrett, Burns Flat, Oklahoma
Charles Geist, West Babylon, New York
Edward D. Geist, Dallas, Texas
William W. Gillett, Jr., Kearney, Missouri
Dr. and Mrs. Jack Good, Lake Forest, Illinois
William H. Grand, Portland, Oregon
Andrea Gray, New York, New York
Mark Greenberg, Bronx, New York
Herman J. Greitzer, Guttenberg, New Jersey
C. W. Guildner, Snohomish, Washington
Lee Gustafson, Dedham, Massachusetts
Siegfried Halus, Medford, Massachusetts
David Y. Hanse, Shippensburg, Pennsylvania
B. W. Hauk, Hicksville, New York
W. P. Hayes, Newport News, Virginia
H. John Heide, Honolulu, Hawaii
Paula Hendrich, New York, New York
Dr. and Mrs. Paul Henkind, New Rochelle, New York
N. N. Inlander, Flossmoor, Illinois
Joseph D. Isaacson, Pound Ridge, New York
Arthur L. Jacobsen, Mamaroneck, New York
W. Kent Johns, Los Gatos, California
David P. Johnson, Oakland, California
Uosis Juodvalkis, Providence, Rhode Island
Lawrence Kasakoff, Chicago, Illinois
Larry Kassian, Edmonton, Canada
Yoshinobu Kazato, Kawasaki-Shi, Japan
R. A. B. Keates and T. L. Boese, Guelph, Canada
Michael Kenward, West Sussex, England
Ernie Kerr, West Hills, Canada
Richard Klein, Miami, Florida
Harold W. Klinger, La Grange, Illinois
John B. Koegel, New York, New York
Paul E. Kolonay, United States Embassy, Israel
C. C. Korvin, Vancouver, Canada
Roland M. Kriegel, Ridgewood, New Jersey
Kwitoslawa Kulczyky, Chicago, Illinois
Richard Kurtz, New York, New York
Ronald Kurtz, Englewood, New Jersey
Mr. and Mrs. Clyde F. Lambert, Sante Fe, New Mexico
E. Clyde Lambert, Memphis, Tennessee
Erik Lambert, Paris, France
Dr. Emery Lane, Louisville, Kentucky
Debbie Larson, Dallas, Texas
Lindon G. Leader, Studio City, California
Trevor Leak, Jeddah, Saudi Arabia
Dr. Gordon E. Lee, Glenwood, Minnesota
Russell Lee, Austin, Texas
Eleanor Lewis, Thetford Hills, Vermont
Dawson Lim, Pittsburgh, Pennsylvania
Clifford Love, Nashville, Tennessee
Phoebe Franklin Lundeen, Atlanta, Georgia
David Hunter McAlpin, Princeton, New Jersey
Barry McCormick, Riverside, Connecticut
Gary McIntyre, Hofheim, West Germany
Phillippe McIntyre, Falls Church, Virginia
Taylor McKelvey, Atlanta, Georgia
Matthew M. McKenna, New York, New York
Brockway McMillen, Sedgewick, Maine
Richard G. Mack, Louisville, Kentucky
Ben Maddow, Los Angeles, California
Dr. Stephen D. Maegin, Leonia, New Jersey
Christian Malize, New York, New York
Ronald E. Mallen, San Francisco, California
Robert Mancuso, Barrington, Illinois
Gerald R. Martin, Richfield, Minnesota
Linda Martyntak, New Orleans, Louisiana
Philip Masnick, New York, New York
Cloyd Massengill, Oakland, California
Rowland L. Matteson, Chicago, Illinois
Neil E. Matthew, Indianapolis, Indiana
Dr. Wesley L. Mayo, Bridgeport, Connecticut
Rosario Mazzeo, Carmel, California
Michael D. Melet, Flint, Michigan
Alan Michalka, West Milford, New Jersey
David H. Miller, New York, New York
John A. Mirabelli, Lindenhurst, New Jersey
David Molchos, Miami, Florida
Roger P. Mulligan, Blind River, Canada
Robert A. Murrone, Bronx, New York
Tad Nichols, Tucson, Arizona
David C. Olivetti, Ivrea, Italy
Daniel J. O'Brien, Oak Lawn, Illinois
G. Oppenheimer, Jerusalem, Israel
Mrs. Leo Panasevich, Weston, Massachusetts
Alan C. Parker, Jefferson, Louisiana
Douglas Todd Parker, Stamford, Connecticut
Photo Pictorial, Hong Kong
Eliot F. Porter, Santa Fe, New Mexico
Kevin Power, Brard, France
Herb Quick, Riverside, California
Marcia Raff, Columbus, Georgia
C. W. Reiquam, Lakewood, Colorado
James Resendiz, Chicago, Illinois
B. Resnick, Melville, New York
Nicholas F. Rizzo, Jr., Brooklyn, New York
Lynn P. Roberts, Ossining, New York
Victoria Ruder, Boston, Massachusetts
R. Michael Ruppert, Sherman Oaks, California
David C. Ruttenberg, Chicago, Illinois
Mario Samarughi, Rome, Italy
Carlos M. Santoyo, Arlington, Virginia
Michael E. and Michael Grant Scala, Rumford, Rhode Island
Gerald Schnitzer, Fort Lauderdale, Florida
Dennis Schubert, Santa Ana, California
Barney Sellers, Columbia, Maryland
Lawrence M. Sentner, Albuquerque, New Mexico
Daniel Shever, New York, New York
Rocky Shugart, Houston, Texas
Jim Sipes, Daly City, California
Dr. David Slaughter, Montreal, Canada
Jane Talmadge Smith, Venice, California
Joseph A. Snook, Kutztown, Pennsylvania
James L. Sockwriter, Knoxville, Iowa
Abigail Solomon-Godeau, New York, New York
Joe Sonneman, Juneau, Alaska
Gregory B. Soos, Huntington Beach, California
Arthur B. Steinman, West Nyack, New York
Frederick Stone, Cambridge, Massachusetts
Jay Strickland, Rock Island, Illinois
Charles K. Strowd, Jr., Chapel Hill, North Carolina
Gray W. Stuart, Austin, Texas
Ellen D. Sturgis, Minneapolis, Minnesota
R. B. Thornton, Montreal, Canada
Peter G. Thorpe, APO New York
Charles Tompkins, Washington, Virginia
Laurie Triplette, Winston-Salem, North Carolina
Fred J. Turner, Jr., Newtown Square, Pennsylvania
Norman H. Ursel, Vancouver, Canada
James J. Vanecko, Brookline, Massachusetts
Sarita Van Vleck, Captiva, Florida
W. J. Van Wagtendonk, Cedar Mountains, North Carolina
Jens Vossman, Linsburg, West Germany
Wach Gallery, Avon Lake, Ohio
Bruce J. Walsh, La Salle, Illinois
Richard and Barbara Wamboldt, Pasadena, California
Alex H. Warner, Boulder, Colorado
Fred Wedel, Anchorage, Alaska
Matthew J. Wells, Randolph, Massachusetts
Frank R. Wendtlandt, Leawood, Kansas
Thomas Weski, Hanover, West Germany
David N. Whitson, LaGrande, Oregon
Herbert F. Wilkinson, Oakland, California
Arthur J. Williams, New York, New York
Edward J. Williams, Albuquerque, New Mexico
David R. Wilson, Rochester, New York
Diana Wold, Miami, Florida
Lucia Woods and Dan Lindley, Evanston, Illinois
Robert Worth, Upper Montclair, New Jersey
Lulu and Yoshi Yoshihara, Denman Island, Canada
Gary S. Yost, San Jose, California
Steve Zwerling, Nova Scotia, Canada
Stephen R. Zylstra, Silverado, California

3700